D1493262

PUBLICATIONS OF THE UNIVERSITY OF MANCHESTER

No. CCXLVII

HISTORICAL SERIES NO. LXXI

THE SERJEANTS OF THE PEACE
IN
MEDIEVAL ENGLAND AND WALES

Published by the University of Manchester at
THE UNIVERSITY PRESS (H. M. McKechnie, M.A., Secretary)
8-10, Wright Street, MANCHESTER, 15

THE SERJEANTS OF THE PEACE

IN

MEDIEVAL ENGLAND AND WALES

BY

R. STEWART-BROWN

M.A., F.S.A.

MANCHESTER UNIVERSITY PRESS

1936

CONTENTS

CONTENTS

PREFACE

THE widespread system of preserving the peace by means of an organization of special peace officers, sometimes holding by hereditary serjeanty, which existed in certain parts of England and in Wales in medieval times, seems to have escaped the notice of the standard writers of constitutional and legal history. So far as can be discovered, neither Stubbs nor Maitland [1] observed it, nor have those who have specially studied the history of the criminal law [2] or that of the justices of the peace.[3] The writers of the *History of English Law before the Reign of Edward I* make the sweeping statement that in the period which they cover " there is no professional police force " [4] ; and though this is qualified by reference to the duties to arrest malefactors incumbent on the sheriff and his bailiffs and those of lords with higher regalities, the special organization of the serjeants of the peace seems not to have been noticed. In his various studies of royal and other serjeanties, Round does not mention those of the peace. Nor are the serjeants referred to in Professor Sir William Holdsworth's recent treatise on the general history of English law. This silence on all sides may in part be due to unobservance of the *servientes pacis*, who are disclosed by a close examination only of the records of county history ; and to the fact that, though perhaps occasionally covered under the general title of *ballivi* of the King or the sheriff, there is no direct mention of them in such landmarks in the history of the

---

[1] Maitland seems to have noticed only the Shropshire serjeants (see p. 67, footnote 1).

[2] *e.g.* Stephen, *Hist. of the Criminal Law* (1883).

[3] *e.g.* Miss Putnam's numerous studies (see p. 141) ; and C. A. Beard, *The Office of Justice of the Peace in England in its Origin and Development* (Columbia University Studies in History, etc., vol. xx, 1904), where the early history of the police system preceding the introduction of the justices was investigated.

[4] *op. cit.*, 2nd ed., ii, 582. Cf. also i, 476, where the statement of Brunner, that outlawry is the sentence of death pronounced by a community which has no police constables, is quoted with approval and applied to outlawry in English law ; and Holdsworth, *Hist. of Eng. Law*, ii, 197, where in writing of the state of the law at the beginning of the thirteenth century, he speaks of a government which is as yet new and has no force of police to assist it.

administration of justice and the preservation of law and order as the assize of Clarendon (1166), the inquest of sheriffs (1170), the assize of Northampton (1176), the proclamation of Archbishop Walter for the preservation of the peace (1195), *Magna Carta*, the writ of 1252 enforcing watch and ward, the Statute of Wales (1284), and the Statute of Winchester (1285). The serjeants of the peace are also entirely ignored in the treatises of the early writers on legal and constitutional history. Nor does Bracton seem to notice them, though they were in his day more or less active peace officers of the sheriff in Lancashire, Cumberland, Westmorland and Northumberland, counties where he sat as a justice in eyre in 1246. Bracton is but one among the long list of legal writers and historians from the earliest times down to that of Palgrave (1832), by whom, in the assumption that the communal system of preserving the peace by tithings of neighbours was everywhere in force, the serjeants of the peace were strangely passed over. Even when it became plain that frankpledge was by no means universal, it does not appear that those who specially studied that system, or indeed anyone, considered how and by what practical method the peace was preserved in areas where the tithing was not known.

The serjeants of the peace have not, however, escaped all notice. They have been observed, without collective treatment, in the local history of Cheshire [1] and Lancashire,[2] and also in Wales,[3] but those who have noticed them seem seldom, if at all, aware that the organization existed outside the immediate area with which they were dealing. Nearly thirty years ago I included a very brief outline of the Cheshire system only in an account of the Hundred Court of Wirral.[4] More recently, Mr. Jolliffe, in an essay on Northumbrian institutions,[5] touched upon the serjeants of the peace, mainly in regard to the antiquity of the ministerial services to which they were entitled, but the existence of the organization outside Northumbrian regions and Wales seems to have been unknown to him. Professor Morris,

---

[1] *e.g.* by Ormerod in his *History of Cheshire,* orig. ed. (1819), vol. ii, p. 52, and see below.
[2] *e.g.* by Harland, *Mamecestre* (Cheth. Soc.) ; Farrer, *Lancs. Pipe Rolls* and elsewhere ; Professor James Tait, *Mediæval Manchester* ; the Rev. T. C. Porteus, the *Hundred of Leyland* (Cheth. Soc.) ; the *Victoria Hist. of Lancs.*
[3] See the books cited below, in chapter II.
[4] *The Wapentake of Wirral,* 1907. The first chapter is full of errors and should be ignored.
[5] *Eng. Hist. Review,* vol. 41. See *post,* p. 90, for some observations on his views.

in *The Frankpledge System* (1910), makes no reference to the serjeants of the peace, but in his work on *The Medieval English Sheriff* (1927), he noted that the sheriff had under him officials employed in making distraints and summonses, and that this duty had sometimes been performed in the twelfth century by the holders of serjeanties, of which he gives some examples, but without treating of the special organization as a whole.[1] Professor Morris's book has, however, made it unnecessary to consider here the functions of the sheriff as the official ultimately responsible for the activities of the serjeants of the peace. Such reference to the system in Cheshire as was quite recently made by Professor Hazeltine was, as he stated,[2] based on my earlier outline mentioned above. The present study, a more extensive investigation of the subject, is due to Professor Hazeltine's suggestion [3] that the history of the serjeants of the peace should be carefully examined.

In an illuminating outline of the many problems involved in the history and development of the commission of the peace, Professor Hazeltine has pointed out that they cannot be solved by taking into account only those officers who bore the title of justices of the peace, and that since the history of the justices involves that of the institutions which they gradually displaced or modified, intensive studies of the early communal, feudal, franchisal and royal authorities charged with the duty of preserving the peace are necessary to secure a complete historical picture. Some of these early institutions have already received, or are in course of receiving, such special treatment ; for example, frankpledge in the works of Dr. Liebermann and Professor W. A. Morris, the functions in regard to the peace of the medieval sheriff in the study by the latter writer, the keepers of the peace in those of Dr. Bertha H. Putnam, and leet jurisdiction in the monograph by Professor Hearnshaw. For these, and similar detailed studies, their writers have had before them, in greater or lesser degree, for comparison, correction and amplification, the views and conclusions of a lengthy list of earlier constitutional and legal writers and historians. In the investigation which has been here attempted such advantages are entirely lacking. The subject is a new one and has had to be treated as such. This book is therefore of a pioneer nature and, primarily,

---

[1] *op. cit.*, 190.
[2] In his General Preface to Dowdell, *A Hundred Years of Quarter Sessions*, 1932, pp. xix-xx n.
[3] *Ib.*, xxx n.

one of research, to which some limits had to be set. There are further investigations to be made, and there remain many questions to be discussed and answered. Such conclusions as have been hazarded here upon the obscure origin of the organization of serjeants of the peace, and its contrast with that of frank-pledge, are of a tentative nature. If they do not meet with acceptance, I shall be satisfied to have provided some materials and sources for the further study of an overlooked institution of some interest and importance in constitutional and legal history. I may be thought to have over-emphasized the institutional side of the matter and placed on record facts which may appear to some to have only an archaeological or antiquarian interest. I have done so because, in a preliminary survey such as this, it is hard to see what facts and data will, or will not, be material for the purposes of ultimate inference and conclusion. For much the same reasons, and to support the statements in the text, I have thought it advisable to give, in an Appendix, a selection of documents illustrating the system and its main features. They will be found to be arranged under regional headings, with cross-references to and from the text, and the sources are indicated in all cases. The documents included for Cheshire, Wales, Lancashire and Shropshire seem fairly representative and fewer have been given for the other areas where the serjeants have been found. The latter have, for the same · reason, received less full treatment in the text itself.

While I am alone responsible for the contents of this book, I wish to acknowledge with gratitude that Professor Hazeltine was good enough to read and comment upon part of my work in its early form, and to obtain for me the remarks upon it of an authority on medieval constitutional history, by all of which I have endeavoured to benefit. I am also indebted to Professor James Tait, Dr. Bertha H. Putnam and Miss M. H. Dodds for information and suggestions and to Professor Ifor Williams for the substance of the note (p. 46) upon the word *cais*, the curious title given to the Welsh serjeant of the peace.

R. S.-B.

April, 1936.

OUTLINE

CHAPTER I will contain an account of the serjeants of the peace in Cheshire and the organizations in this palatine county will be dealt with in some detail. The peace officers included the county serjeants, those of one of the hundreds, those of the forests, the baronies and the franchises. The functions of the normal officers of the hundreds will be examined in relation to those of the peace. The duties and rights of the serjeants will be explained and the decline of the system traced to its practical supersession by the special commissions and the appointments of conservators of the peace. The late introduction into Cheshire of the justices of the peace in 1536 will be dealt with in Appendix I. Chapter II will demonstrate the existence of the system in Wales and the Marches, a very brief note on the institution there, at the same date as in Cheshire, of the justices of the peace being given in Appendix II. An account of the somewhat similar organizations in northern areas (Lancashire, Westmorland, Cumberland, Durham and Northumberland) will follow in Chapter III, but this will not include the keepers, the conservators or the justices of the peace, whose history for these counties runs parallel with that of those institutions elsewhere in England. Chapter IV will contain notes on the system in Shropshire and its borders. Its existence in Herefordshire and the Southern Marches will have been shown in Chapter II. In Chapter V some account will be given of a military type of serjeant of the peace appointed in other counties in the late twelfth and early thirteenth centuries. Some special features of the system will be examined in Chapter VI, including the serjeants' powers of arrest, the part which they played in the presentment of crime, the puture system and the service of " bode and witnessman." Some suggestions upon the origin of the organization, which has been found only in non-frankpledge areas, will be hazarded in Chapter VII, and this will be followed in the final chapter by a contrast and comparison of its features with those of the frankpledge system operating elsewhere. Some illustrative documents are set out in Appendix III.

CHAPTER I

THE SERJEANTS OF THE PEACE IN CHESHIRE

IT has recently been pointed out that an examination of the
historical development, in all directions, of the office of justice
of the peace is needed; and that among the special studies
which, to that end, should be undertaken, would be one devoted
to the systems adopted in the great palatinates for the preservation of the peace.   Such an investigation would, it was suggested,
involve the history of institutions which the adoption of a
regular system of justices of the peace modified or displaced,
and of any feudal and franchisal authorities which had previously
been charged with such duties.[1]   The study here attempted, so
far as it concerns the palatinate of Chester, falls somewhat short
of this ideal, which would indeed call for the writing of a new
history of the county, a work yet to be undertaken.   It will
be confined to an account of the practical methods by which
the earls, Norman and royal, attempted to prevent crime and
to bring offenders to book, down to the dates in the sixteenth
century when the justice of the peace emerged, first for the
city, and later for the county, of Chester.   The history of the
palatine courts [2] (not assimilated to those of the kingdom until
1830), and those of the baronial franchises, as well as of other
institutions peculiar to this palatinate, requires separate treatment, and these will only incidentally be touched on here so
far as they seem immediately material for a study to which
some limits must be set.   The system devised for the preservation of the peace and the maintenance of order in Cheshire and
also in Wales deserves special attention, if only for the reason
that the introduction of the justice of the peace (*eo nomine* at
any rate), which is considered to have occurred elsewhere during
the fourteenth century, did not take effect in these areas until
nearly the middle of the sixteenth century.

   When, after a short period in the hands of Gherbod as chief

[1] Professor Hazeltine, *loc. cit.*
[2] For some account of these in the thirteenth century, see my introduction to *Calendar of Chester County Court Rolls* (Cheth. Soc.).

representative of the Conqueror, the control of Cheshire as a border buffer against the Welsh was in 1071 entrusted, with absolute control, to Earl Hugh of Avranches, he seems to have been given a free hand, either to adapt to his purpose such local institutions as he found surviving and suitable, or to introduce, with modifications, such new ones as the experience of the Normans in their own realms had proved useful and effective. The permanent maintenance of a sufficient number of men to fight the Welsh was secured by the earl mainly through grants of land and rights of jurisdiction to a small body of trusted persons who became his " barons," and by sub-infeudations provided their own military quotas.[1] This form of delegation of jurisdiction with its profits, coupled with military duties and police obligations, was doubtless familiar to the Normans in their own country and was readily adaptable to the necessities of a county where something of the same kind was known before the conquest.[2]

Among the organizations which are found in existence is the one it is proposed to examine, that for the preservation within the county of the earl's peace. In accordance with a decision to omit some of the various agencies which contributed to such an object, the functions of the justiciar of Chester, doubtless an ex-officio *custos pacis*,[3] will not be discussed. Nor will much be said of the sheriff who, in Cheshire, was apparently always a minor administrative officer subordinate to the justiciar, with judicial functions and official powers of inferior importance.[4] The coroners as peace officers in Cheshire seem also to have played only a minor rôle.[5] Those of the hundreds and the city of Chester are found making presentments of crime in the thirteenth century [6] and later, but, as elsewhere, that one of all their original duties which comprised the apprehension of accused persons seems to have fallen away, and in the fourteenth century it appears to have been necessary to give both them and the sheriff special commissions for this purpose,[7] which would hardly have been required if they had the full powers of *custodes pacis*. The chamberlain (the chancellor) as a *custos*

[1] See the section on the military service of Cheshire in *Cal. Chester County Court Rolls*, xliii.

[2] Cf. Haskins, *Norman Institutions*, 24, etc., Reid, " Barony and Thanage " (*Eng. Hist. Review*, 35, 1920, p. 167).

[3] For some account of this official, see *Cal. Chester County Court Rolls*, p. xix.

[4] *Ib.*, p. xxvi. (For the normal sheriff, see Morris, *The Mediaeval English Sheriff*.)

[5] *Ib.*, p. xxviii.   [6] *Ib.*, p. xli.   [7] *Post*, p. 30.

pacis will be mentioned in a later portion of the present study.[1]

Another matter of some interest in connection with the subject is one which has been discussed elsewhere,[2] namely, the avowry system in Cheshire, possibly derived from Welsh sources. Under this, felons and wrongdoers, as well as innocent persons coming from other parts, could, by payment of an annual fee and on certain conditions, obtain the protection of the earl, or of such of his " barons " as had the privilege, against the consequences of crime. Some degree of control over transgressors of the peace and potential criminals was thus exercised, but the system was vicious, and resulted in the admission, and harbouring, within the county, of large numbers of the criminal classes, which must have greatly increased the difficulties of preserving the peace. Beyond noting this aspect of it, there is no need here to take the avowry system into account.

(a) The County Serjeants of the Peace

For the preservation of the earl's peace in Cheshire there existed, in the first place, a hereditary office of grand serjeanty, called the " Master Serjeanty of the Peace " (*magisterialis serjeantia pacis*) for the county. In the holder of this office may be discerned an early type of *custos pacis*, the forbear, in some respects, of the justice of the peace. It is possible, though the evidence is only inferential, that the first holder of this office in Cheshire was Robert fitz Hugh, the " baron " of Malpas, named first in the Domesday list of the earl's chief men as the holder of twenty-nine manors out of a total of three hundred and thirty-eight, the earl retaining forty-eight as his own demesne.[3] It is certain that the serjeanty descended hereditarily in the line of one of his two daughters (though neither of their husbands can as yet be shown to have held it) ; and it is possible, though there is some later evidence against it, that the duties were considered as impartible on his death, and so have been allotted with that part of the lands and obligations attaching to the fee of Malpas which was apportioned to the elder of two heiresses, for performance by her husband.[4] When, upon the annexation of the earldom to the crown in 1237, the revenues of the county appear upon the Pipe Rolls, the debits of the *custos* John de Lacy, earl of Lincoln, between June 1237

[1] p. 27.   [2] *Eng. Hist. Review*, 29, 1914.
[3] Tait, *Domesday Survey of Cheshire*, p. 30.
[4] On the impartibility of serjeanties, see Round, *The King's Serjeants.*

and August 1238, include a payment of 60s., probably for robes, to Robert de Cholmondeley and Owin, with their associates, keeping the King's peace during the year in Cheshire.[1] Cholmondeley was a descendant of Robert fitz Hugh the " baron " of Malpas, and he and Owin were probably deputy-master-serjeants of the peace, in which capacity another Cholmondeley served later.[2] The descent of the " barony " of Malpas and the earlier pedigree are very uncertain, but it seems clear that some time in the thirteenth century the undivided county serjeanty was in the hands of David de Malpas " the bastard," as the husbands of his two daughters, Rhodri ap Gruffydd and Urian de St. Pierre, held the serjeanty jointly in right of their wives towards the end of that century, and the subsequent holders until the office ceased to exist, the Suttons and St. Pierres, were their respective descendants.[3]

The paucity of early records makes it difficult to trace the serjeanty backward, but its existence in the twelfth century can inferentially be shown by the records of the customary payments made out of the revenues of the earldom to the master serjeants or their men for the head of each robber decapitated by their men and brought to Chester castle. The Pipe Rolls from 1181, when Hugh Kevelioc earl of Chester died, to 1187, when his son Randle Blundeville came into his full inheritance as earl, often disclose, among the items disbursed from the revenue of the earldom, annual payments of a few shillings *pro justicia facienda de raptoribus*.[4] When the Pipe Roll entries of the issues of Cheshire next reappear in 1237–38 so do these serjeants' fees, and again in many subsequent years.[5]

Under the master serjeant there seem to have been originally twenty county serjeants of the peace, and acting with them, under the sheriff, a staff of assistants, sometimes called bedells

---

[1] Appendix III, no. 1.

[2] Ormerod, *Hist. of Cheshire*, ed. Helsby, vol. ii, p. 630.

[3] *Ib.*, ii, 109, 595, etc. The *inq. p.m.* of Urian de St. Pierre, 1294–96, shows he had a moiety of the serjeanty of the peace, by the courtesy of England, by finding 10 [half the original 20] serjeants to keep the peace within the county and received 30s. at the exchequer of Chester for cloaks (*mantellis*) of his men (*Cal. Inq.*, P.R.O., iii, nos. 280, 376 ; see also v, no. 251). The *inq.*, 1290, of Beatrice wife of Roderic Griffin (sister of the wife of St. Pierre) mentions her [moiety of] the serjeanty, with 10 marks a year (*ib.*, ii, no. 749).

[4] Appendix III, no. 1. Cf. Farrer, *Lancs. Pipe Rolls*, pp. 187, 199, 213, 220, 228, Cannon, *Pipe Roll 1241–42*, p. 19 (Shropshire), for payments apparently similar but occasionally covering other items.

[5] See also the fourteenth-cent. payments in the *Cheshire Chamberlains' Accounts* (*Rec. Soc. Lancs. and Chesh.*).

of the peace, and doubtless numerous underlings. The master serjeant certainly and probably some of his serjeants, were mounted, the more easily to perform their duty. This involved the perambulation of all the hundreds of the county, with the exception, at any rate in the thirteenth century, of those of Wirral and Macclesfield. The former (the Domesday hundred of Wilaveston) was, probably in the late eleventh or early twelfth century, created one of the earl's forests and so remained until 1376. Portions of Macclesfield Hundred (the Hamestan of Domesday) were also included in the forest areas and the manor of Macclesfield itself was part of the earl's demesnes. Special arrangements for these two hundreds were made, to which reference will be made later on.

Whether the disciplinary visitations of the earl's serjeants of the peace ever normally extended into the demesne manors of his " barons " is uncertain, but it will be found that the latter had their own organization of serjeants, acting supplementarily, and in some respects subordinately, to those of the earl, within their own fees, but with powers not quite so plenary. The county serjeants, if they had to enter a barony, were probably accompanied by the baronial officers, and if the " baron " had *retorna brevium* the jurisdiction of the county serjeants seems to have been entirely excluded.

The earl's serjeants and the bedells travelled through the hundreds, taking cognizance of all offences against the peace and keeping watch. The serjeants had very full powers of arrest, including the ancient right to behead a robber instantly if caught in the act or if sufficient evidence against him was immediately forthcoming. For each robber's head taken to the castle at Chester a shilling fee was obtained, with two shillings and sometimes a salmon, if in season, for that of a master robber.[1] For other actual or suspected offences arrests were made or information laid, leading to presentments at the hundred courts, for trial by the earl's justiciar (not the sheriff) in the hundred " eyres " and the county court. In the wapentakes of Lancashire the master serjeants of the peace seem to have paid an annual fee, but the county master serjeant in Cheshire does not appear to have done so. There are indications of an exchequer allowance of 30s. for clothing the officers in Cheshire. They were remunerated by perquisites and free quarters, and in early days by a small fee, perhaps the allowance just mentioned. A

[1] *Ante*, p. 4 ; Ormerod, ii, 109, 595 ; iii, 62 ; and *Chesh. Chamberlains' Accts.*, 6, 24, 86, 93.

proportion of the goods and chattels of felons and outlaws forfeited to the earl (or to a " baron " who had the right to such
" waif " (*vaga*)) was the perquisite of the serjeants and bedells
who seized such goods, as a stimulus to activity, under the
term " pelf." For this they took, according to some accounts,[1]
the felon's best beast of each kind, all wooden vessels, linen and
woollen clothes, a quarter of any threshed corn, and all the
money if it did not exceed five pounds. Everything made or
bound with iron went with the residue of the felon's goods to
Chester castle for the earl. Deodands and the goods of suicides
seem also to have been perquisites of the serjeanty. " Pelf "
was only claimable by the serjeants if they could take possession
of the goods of the felon before the sheriff or the coroner of the
hundred had seized and placed them in the custody of the township of the felon or fugitive.[2]

In addition to their police duties proper, the serjeants and
bedells made proclamations, carried the earl's messages, attended,
apparently under the sheriff, to the execution of attachments
and distraints of the county court, and served writs and official
notices ; though all these duties were evidently in many cases
forced upon others, as complaints testify.[3]

The activities of the peace officers are not very readily
visible in the records of the trial and conviction of an offender.
They had arrested him or obtained evidence of the crime, and
they had arranged for such evidence, in the shape of witnesses
or local gossip, to be presented to the court by representatives
of the vicinity or by inquisition. When this had been done
their duties were over and there only remained the collection
of the profits arising out of their activities when in due course
the offender was amerced, outlawed or otherwise condemned.[4]

It is not clear whether the maintenance of the peace serjeants,
together with their horses and retinue, called " puture " (*putura*),[5]

---

[1] *The Wapentake of Wirral*, 31, and references there given ; *Cal.
Chester County Court Rolls*, 141.
[2] For a fourteenth-cent. dispute about this, see Appendix III, no. 2.
An appointment in 1356 of an official vendor of felons' goods at a salary
of 60s. a year, the serjeants not to take more than a quarter of the threshed
corn, is on record (*Cal. Chesh. Recog. Rolls, 36 Rep. Dep. Keeper*, 108).
[3] Below, p. 9.
[4] *Cal. Chester County Court Rolls, passim ;* also the lists of amercements and forfeitures in county court or hundred eyre in *Chesh. Chamberlains' Accts.*, 50 *sqq.* Most offences were punished by fines, few with
death, in these times. It is probable that an examination of the later
unprinted county court and eyre rolls of Cheshire might throw more light
on this matter.
[5] See below, p. 81.

was originally thrown upon the hundreds of Cheshire or upon a class of freemen ; but when evidence begins it appears as a tenurial obligation lying upon certain only of the residents in a periodical rotation. Their holdings are often given the name of " warlands." This term is applied in Domesday Book to lands which " defended " or exonerated other areas from payment of geld by taking over the liability and having their own assessments increased ; and it is a fair presumption that later on " warlands " was used as the name for lands which assumed responsibility for other renders or payments,[1] and, in relation to the serjeants' " puture," were those holdings in a hundred upon which somehow had fallen this obligation.[2] It would seem indeed that only from such holdings or " warlands " could " puture " be exacted. There is some evidence that a " warland " must have comprised at least an acre, and that, for the forest serjeants at any rate, puture could not be demanded from holders of less.[3] Payment in kind, such as food, drink, oats, dogs' meat, and so on, constituted the original puture, but in course of time this was commuted to a money payment of a few shillings a year collected on behalf of the officers.

During their rounds the serjeants were obliged to take " pot luck," but although they ought to have demanded only such food as happened to be in the house, they frequently called for more than this, thus abusing the right of puture. Only two serjeants (not counting the master serjeant if he were out with them), with two attendants, could claim to be billeted upon a single holding ; and after a supper, a night's rest, and a morning meal, they had to move on, leaving the houses visited free

[1] *The Wapentake of Wirral*, 18.
[2] *Le warlond ejusdem manerii* [Norcliffe] *tenetur pascere servientes domine regine de Maklesfeld de mense in mensem quolibet mense per unam diem* (Inq. of Thos. de Orreby 18 Ed. 1. *Cal. Inq.*, vol. ii, 762) ; the service from the manor of Cheadle included puture for the serjeants of Macclesfield every month from the forinsic lands of the manor (*ib.*, vol. iii, p. 99) ; the serjeants of the baron of Halton had puture, or a reasonable payment instead, from all tenants holding *tres landas terrae vel plures terrarum vocatarum warland infra feodum* (Ormerod, i, 704) ; the forester of Mara and Mondrem claimed puture from everyone holding a " meese " and three selions of land, ware land (which contain an acre), but not when the holding was less than one acre (*ib.*, ii, 109) ; the baron of Dunham Mascy claimed puture for his serjeants from tenants who held *terra puturae* (*ib.*, i, 526) ; feeding one bedell once in six weeks was part of the service of lands in Barterton (*Cal. Inq.*, ii, no. 460) ; puture for the serjeants of the peace and for the sheriff's bedells was due from Waverton (*ib.*, no. 782) ; Weston, Kekewick and Preston owed puture for the serjeants of the baron of Halton, with provender for his master serjeant's horse (*ib.*, iii, no. 220).
[3] Ormerod, ii, 109.

from a similar call until on the system of rotation their turn came round again.

That this obligation is found to have lain upon some of the lands given to the religious houses points to its antiquity ; and in course of time most of them succeeded in freeing themselves from it. The abbey of Chester, for example, about the late twelfth century, obtained acquittance from the earl from puture for his peace serjeants in all its lands in the hundred of Wirral, but not from puture for six forest serjeants in this area except in the abbey's four demesne manors of Sutton, Eastham, Bromborough, and Irby, which were freed entirely, whether or not war called for a re-imposition, or an increase in the number, of the peace serjeants.[1] From John, the last Norman earl, the abbey obtained acquittance for four other manors elsewhere in time of peace and for two more entirely.[2] Stanlow and Whalley abbeys received releases of puture on some of their Cheshire estates from both the master serjeant of the peace and the master forester of Delamere themselves.[3] The houses of Combermere, Norton, Dieulacres, Birkenhead [4] and doubtless others, obtained similar acquittance, which was also granted occasionally as a favour to the lay owners of manors, such as the lord of Thornton-le-Moors,[5] and the Fittons at Bollin.[6]

The *Magna Carta* of Cheshire, *c*. 1216, granted by the earl and redressing many grievances of his " barons," provided that for the future there were to be in time of peace only twelve itinerant serjeants instead of twenty, the master serjeant alone to be mounted ; and compulsory exactions of fodder for his horse were not to be taken between Easter and Michaelmas (when grass would be available). The serjeants were to be content with such food as was in the house which they visited, and pay for any specially required. They were not to eat in the " barons' " demesne manors (from which we may infer the exclusion there of their jurisdiction except on special occasions not involving a stay) ; and the exactions of sheaves and presents customarily made by the serjeants and the bedells were to cease. The number of serjeants in time of war was to be settled by the earl with the advice of the " barons " and the justiciar, and was to be sufficient *ad terram meam custodiendam*.[7] There is evidence in the Cheshire Pipe Rolls of occasional increases in numbers.

[1] Appendix III, no. 3.   [2] *Ib.*, no. 4.
[3] *Ib.*, nos. 5 and 6.   [4] *Ib.*, no. 7.   [5] *Ib.*, no. 8.
[6] *Cheshire Sheaf*, iii, vol. 19, p. 16.   [7] Appendix III, no. 9.

As indicated above, the exact relations of the serjeants of the peace with the sheriff and the county and hundred courts are obscure, but for general purposes they and their underlings, the bedells, evidently acted on the sheriff's instructions. Early in the reign of Edward III, about 1331, the " charterers," or freeholders, of the county complained of oppressions and extortions by the bedells of the peace of the earl, also called " serjeants of the chamber," who were at that time clothed by the sheriff. It was alleged that alike in the time of the Norman earls, during the reign of Edward I and up to the time (1309) of Robert de Bulkeleigh, when sheriff, the bedells had served the sheriff's summonses in person, certified by the testimony at court of two freeholders. But subsequently, it was asserted, the bedells had forced the freeholders to serve the summonses, taking fines from them of from a penny to threepence that they should not be sent for this purpose far from home ; while later on, the bedells, growing bolder, not only handed to the freeholders the panels of names directed to them by the sheriff but other panels arbitrarily drawn up, and forced them to serve the summonses both within and without the hundred in which they lived under penalty of a fine for exoneration. The justiciar endeavoured to avoid an inquiry, as he saw that it would tend to a great decrease in the revenue of the sheriff, but he was obliged to hold it. The decision of the jury was that the freeholders were bound by custom to serve the summonses (presumably for juries and inquisitions and the appearance at court of persons under attachment and their sureties) but only in their own hundreds and that the panels were to be limited to twenty-four names ; they could only be called upon to testify to the service at the next sitting of the county court. It was further decided that no one was to be called upon to serve a second summons until all others of that tenure in the hundred had done their turn ; and moreover the bedells of the earl were no longer to take gifts, " thiggyng " (beggings) [1] or " fullenale " (provender),[2] and were only entitled to their puture in the houses of tenants of " warlands." [3] It is during this, the fourteenth, century that the revenues of the hundred courts include sums of money, sometimes called freemen's silver, representing the fines, paid by the " charterers " whose lands did not exceed 40s. in annual

[1] This is more probably the meaning than " thatch " or withies, which I adopted in *The Wapentake of Wirral*, 26.

[2] Cf. Harland, *Mamecestre*, 303.

[3] Inq. 5 Ed. III, in *Calendar of Chesh. Plea Rolls, 28th Report Dep. Keeper*, Appendix 6, p. 25.

value, to avoid the obligation of serving the summonses just mentioned.[1] A statute of 1293,[2] directed to the relief from these duties of persons of small means, had enacted that those empanelled by sheriffs and their officers for such services outside a county should have lands of the value of 100s. and those within a county 40s. This was later modified by an order that former usage should hold respecting common pleas in the eyres and also for juries in cities and towns.[3]

In 1290 the Cheshire organization is mentioned in a noteworthy local protest, made against the application to the county palatine of the statute of Winchester, passed five years earlier. That act was directed against the lawless conditions of the country generally, in which jurors had neglected their duties of presenting the robber, murderer, and felon to justice. In future "fresh suit" must be made against offenders, and inquiries held in town, hundred, franchise, and county. If these failed to produce felons and wrongdoers, the people of the hundred where the offence was committed were to be answerable for the damage. The existence of a special organization of peace officers, both in Cheshire and (as we shall see) elsewhere, whose duties included the pursuit, arrest and presentment of criminals and the seizure of their goods and chattels, was ignored, and the men of Cheshire felt that an undue burden was being thrown upon them by the statute. They presented a petition to the King, pointing out that they were already saddled with the maintenance of the serjeants of the peace and asking for exoneration from the new statutory obligations on the ground that they would thereby be more heavily burdened than the rest of the realm. The royal reply was, however, unaccommodating. It was not the King's intention either to alter the customary organization of the serjeants or to revoke his statute.[4]

(b) THE SERJEANTY IN THE HUNDRED OF MACCLESFIELD

The Master Serjeanty (*magisterialis serjancia*) of the Peace in the Hundred of Macclesfield, wherein lay the earl's demesne manor, was a separate office independent of the county serjeanty, and it must also be distinguished from the Serjeanty of the forests of Macclesfield and Leek. The earliest recorded holder

---

[1] Below, p. 17, and *The Wapentake of Wirral*, 33, etc. For an exemption from carrying or being put on panels, see *Register of the Black Prince*, iii, 250.

[2] *Statutes of the Realm*, i, 113.

[3] *Cal. Close Rolls, 1288–96*, 380–81. [4] Appendix III, no. 10.

of the Hundred serjeanty was Adam de Sutton, but the office
seems to have been taken from him and vested about 1220 [1]
in the Davenport family on special terms mentioned below.
The jurisdiction originally extended as far as the earl's lands
in Leek in Staffordshire.[2] There were eight serjeants, one
mounted, with duties and rights to puture within the hundred
similar to those of the county serjeants of the peace, though
in the early thirteenth century the rights to puture in the
township of Mottram in Longdendale and the fee of Bollin
were released. In 1281 this Davenport serjeanty was described
as " the service of riding through the fees of the King in Cheshire
and those of the Queen in Staffordshire, by reason of her manor
of Macclesfield." The lords of these fees had prevented Roger
de Davenport from executing his office and having puture ;
and accordingly a commission of *oyer* and *terminer* was ordered
to be issued to see that the King had the full service due, that
his peace was kept, and that Roger had his puture in the same
way as his father Vivian.[3]

The office descended regularly in the Davenport family. In
1499 the duties of this master serjeant, such as they then were,
included the proclamation of the peace at fairs, when no one
was allowed to carry lethal arms, a fee of 6*d*. a fair being due.[4]
As late as 1602 there was a dispute [5] on the death of a holder
of the office as to whether it was held in chief of the earl, and
it was proved by the production of the original charter that
this was not so, the office having been granted free of all other
services, only returning to tenure *in capite* if the holder became
unable or unwilling to perform the duties, which had never
happened. In the possession of the Davenports of to-day there
are lengthy rolls containing the names of robbers beheaded by
their ancestors' men, with notes as to the fees paid for their
heads at Chester castle, as in the case of the county serjeanty,
and particulars of the deodands and perquisites of their hereditary
office which continued to be titularly claimed until the last
century, the nominal serjeanty being included in a partition of
1677 and in a family recovery of 1744–45.[6]

[1] *Ib.*, no. 11 ; *Close Roll*, 28 April 1242.
[2] In 1285 the abbot of Dieulacres claimed that part of the serjeanty
pertained to his manor of Leek (*Cal. Chester County Court Rolls*, 232, 237).
[3] *Cal. Pat. Rolls*, 26 May 1281. Puture was sued for in the county
court in 1260 (*Cal. Chester County Court Rolls*, p. 13).
[4] P.R.O., Chester *Quo Warranto* pleas. For these, see my article in
Eng. Hist. Review, Oct. 1934, and *Cheshire Sheaf*, 1935.
[5] 39 *Rep. Dep. Keeper*, Appendix, 90–91.
[6] Ormerod, iii, 67, and Earwaker, *East Cheshire*, ii, 384.

(c) THE FOREST SERJEANTS

The history of the forests of Cheshire remains to be fully written, though both Ormerod and Earwaker have provided a basis.[1] While the forest serjeants were primarily entrusted with the preservation of " the peace of the beasts," their ruthless performance of the duty of seeing that the forest laws were observed made them, in a sense, custodians of the peace, within their jurisdiction, and acted as a great deterrent to poachers, trespassers and other wrongdoers. For these reasons a short account of the forest serjeants seems necessary in an account of the earl's peace system ; but they cannot be said to stand so much in the historical line of the justices of the peace as the county serjeants of the peace.

(1) *The Master Forester of Wirral*

This hundred was placed under a Master Forester (*forestarius ballivæ de Wyrhale*) when it was thrown into the forest towards the end of the eleventh or in the early twelfth century, and the jurisdiction of the county serjeants was seemingly then excluded. The forester was, between 1129 and 1139, endowed by the earl with the manors of Storeton and Puddington, and held his office by the tenure of acting as hereditary master forester, with a horn as his ensign of office, still preserved by the representatives of the Stanley family of Hooton to whom the forestership subsequently descended.[2] Under him a body of forest serjeants perambulated the hundred, their chief duty being the enforcement of the forest law and the presentment of offenders at the eyres. A riding forester, six serjeants, and many attendants, constituted the force in the twelfth century, with rights of puture within the hundred. From one of the Norman earls the freemen of Wirral obtained a charter of acquittance from puture of the serjeants of the peace (which shows that those serjeants had originally perambulated there), but not from puture of the forest serjeants on foot.[3] Attention has already been drawn

---

[1] See also *Ches. Chamberlains' Accts.*, and the *Black Prince's Reg.*, vol. iii. Cox, *The Royal Forests of England*, has notes on the forests of Cheshire. The best accounts of the Norman forest organization are in Petit-Dutaillis, *Studies Supp. to Stubbs' Const. Hist.*, Turner, *Select Pleas of the Forest* (Selden Soc.), and Liebermann, *Constitutiones de Foresta*, 1894.

[2] Ormerod, ii, 355, 446 ; *Black Prince's Reg.*, vol. iii *passim*. The horn is in the possession of the Earl of Cromer, *Picturesque Wirral*, 1912. The original charter is in the John Rylands Library, Stanley Charter 1807, and I have written a paper upon it for the Hist. Soc. of Lancs. and Cheshire.

[3] Appendix III, no. 12.

to the exemptions of the abbot of Chester from puture in this forest, re-stated in this early twelfth-century charter, which further provided that if any business (doubtless of a warlike nature) arose rendering serjeants of the peace necessary there, the men of Wirral should find as many as twelve and maintain them so long as necessary at their own cost. They themselves engaged to do their utmost to defend the earl's land and ensure its peace which they had sworn to observe. They were to maintain the foresters and arrest offenders themselves if possible, handing them over to the earl or to his justice, and making proof of guilt. The necessity for an appointment of a body of such peace serjeants in Wirral in later years does not seem ever to have arisen. Shortly before this hundred was disafforested in 1376,[1] there may have been a nominal serjeant of the peace, but, like those of the county, he was then of small account and we find this office had been included in the rights and profits leased to the " farmers " of the hundred court of Wirral,[2] and gradually it passed into oblivion. The vested rights of the master forester of Wirral to puture money were eventually commuted by private arrangements with the manorial owners by the Stanleys, following upon the charter of disafforestation which had omitted to abrogate these rights.[3] A survival of the franchise of this master forester in 1499 is mentioned below.[4]

(2) *The Master Forester of Macclesfield*

The Master Serjeanty of the forest of Macclesfield with that of the earl's forest of Leek in Staffordshire, was given about 1166 to Richard de Davenport as *supremus forestarius*, and descended in that family. Under him were eight hereditary sub-foresters, bound to their duties by the tenure of their lands, with functions and puture like those of the foresters of Wirral.[5] These sub-serjeanties, and doubtless also all the others, could not lawfully be alienated.[6] The only Cheshire forest eyre rolls in print, so far, are a few for this forest towards the end of the thirteenth century.[7] The forest eyre was then held once

---

[1] See my " Disafforestation of Wirral " (*Trans. Hist. Soc. Lancs. and Chesh.*, vol. 59, p. 165, and vol. 70, p. 139). There are some notes on this forest in Cox, *Royal Forests of England*.

[2] *The Wapentake of Wirral*, 38.

[3] Appendix III, no. 13, and see note 1 above. [4] *Post*, p. 31.

[5] Ormerod, iii, 61, and Earwaker, ii, 3, 379, etc.

[6] *Cal. Chester County Court Rolls*, 229.

[7] Among the Macclesfield eyre rolls in *Cal. Chester County Court Rolls*.

a year by the justiciar of Cheshire or his deputies in conjunction with one of his sittings for the eyre of the Hundreds. The forest serjeants are not much in evidence in the proceedings but they had previously conducted the jury of presentment for the regard of vert and venison, to show them the illegal purprestures and assarts, and provided the information leading to the presentments and indictments for breaches of the forest laws. The " barons' " privilege of claiming the trial of their tenants and men applied here, as in the county court, and the baronial serjeants and bailiffs were thus present at the forest eyres. In 1290 Thomas Davenport, then both the master serjeant of the peace in this hundred, and master forester, had gone with his men to arrest a robber received in the house of the parson of Cheadle, and, as the robber had fled, they seized the parson's horse, whereupon the chaplain, by the latter's order as he said, excommunicated the serjeants. The parson was indicted for contempt and ordered to wage his law *se duodecima manu*, but a settlement was come to.[1]

(3) *The Master Forester of the Forests of Mara and Mondrem* (later Delamere)

Here there was a master forester in fee, with eight perambulating sub-foresters and staff. A very curious account of their perquisites has been preserved.[2] The county serjeants' jurisdiction was not, apparently, excluded in this very large forest area, perhaps because it was intersected with highways and was less wild and more populated than Wirral and Macclesfield and could not, like those forests, be left entirely to the forest officers' control.

(d) MILITARY DUTIES OF THE SERJEANTS OF THE PEACE

It is worthy of note, in regard to the general tenure of serjeanties, that the master serjeanties of the peace in Cheshire and those of its forests, while of the class of grand serjeanties, were coupled with certain definite military obligations to the earl. This is clear from the Cheshire inquest of military service of 1288,[3] which shows that Urian de St. Pierre and Rhodri ap Gruffydd, who then held the county peace serjeanty jointly in right of their wives, were bound in time of war with Wales to serve when summoned by the earl, at their own charges within Cheshire but at his expense beyond the Dee or outside

---

[1] *Cal. Chester County Court Rolls*, 247.   [2] Ormerod, ii, 87, 107, 243.
[3] Appendix III, no. 17.

the county.[1] The same duty applied to the master serjeant of the Hundred of Macclesfield, the master forester of Wirral and the hereditary sub-foresters of Macclesfield (but not to the forester of Delamere), the forest officers being discharged from their local duties while on service. Military service to the earl was not a feature of the mesne peace serjeanties of the " barons " [2] though such officers might, one may suppose, by their own tenure have been bound to serve their immediate lords in war.

(e) THE BAILIFFS AND BEDELLS OF THE HUNDREDS

The early history of the officials of the Cheshire hundreds is difficult and obscure, for want of records. It seems desirable to examine it, so far as possible, though the county organization of serjeants of the peace seems to have been separate. Such evidence as is available begins mainly in the fourteenth century, and chiefly consists of appointments of the bailiffs for each hundred, the details of the revenue of the hundred courts accounted for by the sheriff to the chamberlain, and the enrolment of leases of the office of bedell.[3] The bailiff did not hold his office by serjeanty and frequent appointments to the office occur, sometimes for life. The respective duties of bailiff and bedell of the hundred are difficult to disentangle,[4] as the two offices were often held by the same person, and, in course of time, practically merged as one single " office of bailiff or bedell." The bailiff of the hundred was appointed by the earl under sureties and seems to have been for certain purposes the sheriff's local representative. It is to him that orders affecting the hundred were directed and, as will be shown, he was frequently joined in commissions of arrest and included in the appointments of conservators. Besides seeing to the execution within the hundred of the palatine orders, he apparently also assisted in collecting subsidies and taxes and was frequently in arrear with his payments. Probably neither the bailiff nor the bedell of the hundred is to be linked up with the serjeants of the peace.

The bedell was closely connected with the sheriff and the

---

[1] The usual service for the men of Cheshire was between Lyme on the east and Clwyd on the west.

[2] See below, p. 19.

[3] See *Calendars of Chesh. Recog. Rolls* in *Dep. Keeper's Reports*; and the sheriff's and chamberlain's accounts, some of which I printed in *Chesh. Chamberlains' Accts.*; and the *Wapentake of Wirral*.

[4] The distinction between these offices elsewhere was noted by W. A. Morris, *Mediaeval Eng. Sheriff*, 191 n.

hundred court. His term of office was apparently annual but often continued longer. He may have been elected by the men of the hundred, as, unlike the bailiff, no appointments of bedells (except as lessees of the hundred) are enrolled on the Cheshire records, and there is reason to think that the office could not be refused without special exemption.[1] Thus he may have been, as regards the hundred, the representative of the community, and the bailiff that of the earl. The bedell was probably responsible for summoning the court. In the case of the hundred of Edisbury this was anciently performed by means of messengers from each township, who bore a large oaken ball perforated and slung on a leather thong, the ends of which were fixed on an iron bar. After summoning his township, the messenger was met on the boundary of the next one by another to whom he transferred the summons and the ball, which were sent in this way round the hundred.[2]

There seems to be no Cheshire evidence to throw light upon the question of the presiding officer in the hundred court when it was not farmed. It is unlikely that the sheriff could attend so many hundred courts as judge or steward. The bailiff may have so acted as his office was usually for a term of years. The bedell, if elected annually, is most unlikely to have presided. But when he, or the bailiff, or someone else, took a lease of the hundred, the presiding officer was almost certainly a steward, the lessee becoming the " hundredor."

The bedell (not the bailiff) was responsible to the sheriff for the collection of the normal revenue of the hundred and its court. In some cases he did this merely as an " approver," but by the fourteenth century the much abused system of farming out the right to collect such revenues was firmly established. The leases, usually for a year only in the fourteenth century, generally carried with them only portions of the issues of the hundred, for which a small annual rent was paid. If the bedell or another leased the issues, he became, in effect, " lord " of the hundred. Most of the leases from 1352 to 1820 of the hundred court of Wirral are printed[3] and show that in the fourteenth century the bedell or other lessee who took the

---

[1] *Wapentake of Wirral*, 24.

[2] Ormerod, ii, 4. The service of a freeholder in the royal manor of Shotwick in 1280 was to be summoner of the court and to carry letters relating to the manor everywhere within the bounds of Cheshire. (" The Royal Manor of Shotwick," *Trans. Hist. Soc. Lancs. and Chesh.*, lxiv, 138–39.)

[3] *Wapentake of Wirral*, Appendixes I and II.

bedellaria to farm, kept half of the perquisites, fines and amercements of the hundred court and one third part of the value of the felons' goods (*vaga*). He was also then entitled to keep as part of his farm the puture money still payable, in lieu of the ancient serjeants' maintenance, by the tenants of "warlands" within the hundred, as well as the fines which freeholders whose lands did not exceed 40s. in annual value paid to avoid the obligation of serving jury summonses or acting as jurors throughout the hundred.[1] The bedell also took a perquisite known as *suete de prisone*,[2] a payment liable to great abuse, exacted from persons indicted for misdemeanours for allowing them to remain at large and their property unattached from the date when the bedell received the sheriff's writ until the next sitting of the county court. The balance of the issues of the hundred was accounted for to the sheriff, who in turn accounted to the chamberlain.[3] If the bedell was only an "approver" he accounted for all the revenue. As indicated above, the offices of bailiff and bedell gradually fused, the lessee of the hundred rights sometimes being described as the one or the other. In 1391 and later the lease in the case of the hundred of Wirral was of the *officium bedellarie hundredi* ; in 1445 it was of the *officium ballivi et bedellarie hundredi*. To this lease was added the issues of the sheriff's turn, which, about this time seems to make its first appearance in the history of Cheshire, though without any connection with the system of frankpledge. The lease in 1507 was of all the issues of the bailiwick of the hundred and by 1596 the grant had become one of *totum hundredum*. In 1820 the crown sold by auction the Hundred Court of Wirral, with a number of ancient rights,[4] and the court of this hundred under a "lord" entered upon a scandalous career of exploitation, culminating in its abolition by act of parliament in 1856.[5] The history of the bedells and courts of the other Cheshire hundreds could doubtless be similarly outlined as some documentary evidence is available and the courts seem to have existed into the nineteenth century.[6]

---

[1] *Ante*, p. 10.

[2] See *Wapentake of Wirral*, 34, etc., and my article on "Suete de prisone " in *Eng. Hist. Review*, 24, 1909.

[3] Cf. the sheriff's account of 1349–50, *Chesh. Chamberlains' Accts.*, 134, 136, etc.

[4] These included the fines and amercements in the Hundred Court and sheriff's turn, suit of court, the assizes of bread and ale, treasure trove, waifs, wreck, estrays, goods of felons, deodands and royal fish.

[5] The story is related in detail in *The Wapentake of Wirral*.

[6] See Ormerod, i, 405 ; ii, 4, 585 ; iii, 4, 207, 541.

For the purposes of this investigation it is not necessary to trace the course of the minor civil work performed by the ancient hundred courts but only to notice such features of their criminal or leet jurisdiction as involved the serjeants and bedells of the peace. Their activities as regards these courts, besides a general supervision of the peace in the hundred, must have been mainly concerned with the preparation for the annual " turn " or " eyre " held locally by the justiciar of Cheshire for each of the hundreds, at which presentments and reports of breaches of the peace were made. The desirability and importance of ensuring local knowledge as a means for the effective presentment of crime, where punishment was personal and the preservation of the peace was not controlled by a system of frankpledge, may well be the explanation of the prominence of the bedell in the hundred. Further light doubtless will be available when more of the " eyre " rolls for the hundreds of Cheshire are examined and in print.

An office of serjeant of the hundred occurs but the only two references observed are late and for one of the hundreds only. In 1357 the Black Prince, in view of the prominent part played at the battle of Poictiers by Adam de Acton, sealed an order to the justice and chamberlain of Chester for a grant to him of *la baillie de la serjantie* of the hundred of Bucklow as others had previously held it, provided this involved no detriment to the prince's estate and that good security for due execution of the office was given.[1] In 1363 the same office but called the serjeanty of the peace, was promised for life to John Daniel for long service as one of the prince's archers, with twopence a day as wages, but in 1365, because the office had been abolished by consent of the prince's council for the relief and profit of the common people of the hundred, the pension alone was granted.[2] The existence in the hundreds of a local peace officer seems indicated, but the office does not appear to rank with the hereditary serjeanty of the peace in the hundred of Macclesfield and was probably that of serjeant of the hundred court and may have been abolished for abuses of office. The bedells and the hundred courts in Cheshire, on the other hand, can be kept in view until the nineteenth century and this must largely be due to the fact that the baronial jurisdictions in this county, unlike those of south Lancashire and other parts of the ancient kingdom of

---

[1] Chester Recog. Roll 32–33 Ed. III (Chester 2/41), m. 2 (8) ; *Black Prince's Reg.*, iii, 253.

[2] *Black Prince's Reg.*, iii, 483 and *36 Rep. Dep. Keeper*, 135.

Northumbria, were not coincident with the hundreds, and, though taking away to themselves much of the old jurisdiction of the hundred courts, yet left the latter with enough minor work to keep some of them alive until the nineteenth century.[1]

(f) THE BARONIAL AND FRANCHISAL SERJEANTS OF THE PEACE

Next to be considered are the serjeants of the peace of the feudal jurisdictions, including, in particular, those of the seven or eight magnates classed in Cheshire as " barons," for they also had their own serjeants. The conquest had profoundly changed such jurisdictional areas as may have existed in Cheshire under Earl Edwin of Mercia. Of the three hundred and thirty-eight manors of the Cheshire of Domesday he himself had held twenty, but none of his numerous thegns seems to have held more than sixteen. After the conquest we find Earl Hugh retaining forty-eight manors in his demesne, scattered through most of the hundreds, and distributing a number approaching two hundred among his " barons." Robert fitz Hugh (Malpas) held twenty-nine, the " baron " of Rhuddlan seventeen, Vernon (Shipbrook) fourteen, Malbank (Nantwich) forty-nine, Halton thirty, Dunham about twelve, Kinderton eighteen, with a fief the size of which is not clear held by the " baron " of Mold. More than twenty manors were in the hands of the abbot of Chester who was in status equivalent to a " baron." [2] The delegated privileges granted to these " barons " of taking certain profits of high criminal jurisdiction, which would otherwise have belonged to the earl,[3] naturally involved the obligation to preserve the peace within their manors, and they would be all the more assiduous as by so doing they would increase such profits. To have serjeants of the peace, though not always so called, was usual with all who had the greater franchises of local jurisdiction in Cheshire. Thus subject in some respects to the over-riding powers of the county serjeanty of the peace as regards offenders against the earl's pleas of the sword and the collection of his share of the profits from felons' goods, the " barons " serjeants constituted an additional body of peace officers within limited areas.

The fourteenth-century claim, as " baron " of Halton, by

---

[1] Cf. the cases tried in the last years of the court of Wirral, *Wapentake of Wirral*, p. 120.

[2] Tait, *Domesday Survey of Cheshire*.

[3] *Ante*, p. 2, and, as an example, see the elaborate claims, with detailed explanation of such rights, made by the abbot of Vale Royal in 1350, *Ledger Book of Vale Royal Abbey* (Rec. Soc.), 134, etc.

Henry duke of Lancaster, the constable and marshal of Cheshire, makes this clear.[1] His rights of jurisdiction were of the very highest, only excluding the trial of the earl's pleas of the sword. His court is occasionally called " the hundred " of Halton. He had a master sergeant (*ad equum juratus*), with eight serjeants and two *garciones*, sworn to keep the peace within the fee and to carry out the orders of his courts. The puture system applied to the baronial serjeants and was occasionally relaxed.[2] These serjeants, like those of the county, could at once behead a robber caught in the act within the duke's Cheshire lands, if he admitted his guilt voluntarily before the representatives of four townships, the duke taking the thief's goods and chattels found there. In the case of a felon similarly caught, and whether he confessed or not, the baronial officers had to take him to the duke's prison at Halton, to appear there at three courts if necessary, before the " judicators " and suitors. Here the accused was formally arraigned by the steward and, if he consented to trial there, the inquisition was held ; and if found guilty he was hanged on the gallows of the duke who took his goods and chattels. When the prisoner refused the baronial jurisdiction he was taken off for trial at Chester castle by the earl's justiciar and if convicted there, the baronial serjeants took him back to Halton to be hanged.[3] Whether he was convicted or got off, as so often was the case, by " making fine " with the earl for his peace, the " baron's " rights to the offender's chattels within the fee held good.

The exact line of demarcation between the jurisdiction and functions of the rival serjeants of the earl and of the " baron " is not entirely clear as already observed. Within the barony the earl's serjeants may not have acted after the Cheshire *Magna Carta* of 1216, except in executing or delivering the earl's orders. The respective rights and duties probably came into play according as one or the other effected the original arrest, but even if a county serjeant arrested an offender he could be claimed at

---

[1] Appendix III, no. 18.

[2] *e.g.* the baron of Nantwich released Bertram Griffin from the obligation to feed one bedell once in six weeks at Barterton, *temp*. Henry III. (Ormerod iii, 498 ; *Cal. Inq.*, Ed. I, ii, no. 460. See *ante*, p. 8.)

[3] In 1260 a man arrested by the officers of the " barons " of Nantwich in possession of a stolen horse, asserted that it was his own. As the " barons' " court could not hold an inquisition on this issue, the man was taken to the county court at Chester, charged with theft and ordered to be hanged. The " barons' " bailiffs thereupon claimed him again and he was given up. But because the day was almost spent, a gibbet was lent to them and the thief hanged on the spot instead of on the " barons' " gallows at Nantwich (*Cal. Chester County Court Rolls*, 23).

the county court for trial at the baronial court if the offence
was committed within the " baron's " liberty or the prisoner
was one of his men or tenants.[1] The baronial serjeants, like
those of the county, took " pelf " as a perquisite. The charter
by the " baron " of Halton to the borough of Congleton provided
that, while the bailiffs of the vill were to take arrested felons
to the castle of Halton with any goods found with them, the
bailiffs could keep for themselves the " pelf " which pertained
to the " baron's " serjeanty of the peace.[2]

It seems unnecessary to trace out the other baronial serjeanties in detail. The officers are evident for the " barony "
of Kinderton, where the jurisdictional powers were exercised as
late as 1596, a man arrested for murder being then tried in the
" baron's " court and executed in a field still called the Gallows
field, the executioner probably being provided by the tenant of
" the Hangman's Butts " in Ravenscroft, whose ancient tenure
bound him so to do.[3] The " baron " of Dunham Massey had
six serjeants,[4] the " baron " of Stockport had his,[5] as had the
Audleys, for part of the " barony " of Nantwich,[6] and the
" baron " of Malpas,[7] though in this case there is risk of confusion with those of his county serjeanty of the peace. There
were also the serjeants of those persons of non-baronial rank,
and of monastic bodies, who had been granted similar franchisal
privileges.[8] An example is afforded by the case of the abbey
of Vale Royal, a late foundation by Edward I but with very
full rights and privileges. In 1350 the abbot expressly claimed,

---

[1] For this privilege, see my " Thwert-ut-nay " article in *Eng. Hist.
Review*, 40, 1925.

[2] Ormerod, iii, 36 n.

[3] *Ib.*, iii, 189, 201. For puture of these serjeants, see inquisition of
Ric. Done, 6 Ed. II, *37 Rep. Dep. Keeper*, Appendix, 104.

[4] Appendix III, no. 19.

[5] Ormerod, iii, 790. About 1180–1200 Rob. de Stockport granted to
Rob. de Rumley and his heirs *servientiam feodi mei de Stokeport curiæ
meæ pertinentem*, with a robe annually (Heginbotham, *Stockport*, ii, 296 ;
East Chesh., i, 334).

[6] *Post*, p. 24.   [7] Ormerod, ii, 109, 595, etc.

[8] A reference made by Ducange, *s.v. servientes pacis*, to an instance
of the use of the term in France in a jurisdictional area, may be noted.
He mentions *sergents de la paix banleucæ seu districtus urbis*, and refers
to " Consuet. Valentin. Art. 138." His authority, in fact, is a reference
in " Les Coustumes de la ville, banlieu et cheflieu de Valencienne," decreed
by Charles, Emperor of the Romans, King of Germany, etc., printed in
C. Du Moulin, *Les Coustumes Generales et Particulieres de France et des
Gaules*, 2 vols., fo. 1664. At p. 1128 of vol. ii, cap. 138, shows that
when a man had been wounded, two *sergents de la paix*, with doctors and
surgeons, were sent to inspect and report. It seems doubtful whether
these serjeants were more than the normal *sergents de ville* of a French
town.

among his liberties, that of having serjeants of the peace, and explained that they arrested persons under judgments of his court within his fee, and also disturbers of the peace, taking them to his prison at Weaverham for trial there. Such indeed were the abbot's chartered powers (which included the return of writs) that the county serjeants of the peace had no jurisdiction at all within the abbey liberties.[1] An apparently hereditary office of serjeant of the peace, with custody of the gaol, in the earl's manor or lordship of Frodsham, is mentioned. The duties of this officer included the making of attachments and presentments.[2]

(g) Minor Cheshire Serjeanties

(1) *The Serjeanty of the River Dee*

This serjeanty should be mentioned, as it conferred some minor powers of arrest. It was termed the serjeanty of the waters of the river Dee (*custos ripariæ et aquæ de Dee*) and was held from very early times under the earls of Chester by the predecessors of the Grosvenors. Their master serjeant and his staff controlled the river from Eaton downwards out into the estuary, and had the duty and right of arresting fishermen or others transgressing the ancient rights of the earls by employing improper nets or methods of fishing.[3] In 1506 these functions were vested by charter in the mayor and sheriffs of Chester,[4] but the Grosvenors disputed the rights of the city and continued to exercise the serjeanty until at least 1710, after which it seems to disappear.

(2) *The Serjeants of the Chester City Gates*

There were hereditary serjeants, with duties of guard and of arrest, of some of these gates, *e.g.* the Eastgate, Bridgegate and Watergate, and the custody of the Northgate was in the hands of a keeper appointed by the citizens of Chester. The Watergate was held by grand serjeanty, the duties being to find a man, both in peace and in time of war with Wales, to open and close the gate, and another man, bearing a club, called the serjeant of Watergate Street, to make attachments and dis-

---

[1] *Ledger Book*, 54, 82, 128, 137, 181. In 1357 the abbot complained that, although he had view of frankpledge, the county " hundredors " were drawing his tenants and residents into the hundred courts and amercing them for breaches of articles of the view. *Black Prince's Reg.*, iii, 244.

[2] Ormerod, ii, 51.   [3] *Jour. Chester Arch. Soc.*, i (O.S.), 239, etc.

[4] Morris, *Chester*, etc., 529.

traints within the city. The keeper of the Northgate also had charge of the earl's prison, the pillory and stocks, he executed felons and robbers, and published the earl's proclamations.[1]

(h) THE DECLINE OF THE SYSTEM IN CHESHIRE

It is now possible to visualize the police system devised by medieval ideas for the preservation of the peace in Cheshire, upon which the annexation of the earldom to the crown in 1237 had no effect.[2] It was applied to every part of the county, and, in theory, taking together the earl's county and hundred officers, those of the large forest areas, and of the " barons " and other high jurisdictions, there should have been a sufficient body of duly-warranted serjeants and bedells to effect the purpose of preventing, detecting and bringing to punishment the commission of crime. But in practice things must have been very different. The system was only suited to the rough-and-ready conceptions of law, order and justice of a highly feudalized community. Its defects are easily discerned : the want of any centralized control ; the hereditary and unassignable nature of the master serjeanties ; overlapping jurisdictions with local jealousies ; remuneration based on results ; maintenance imposed by exactions ; exemptions of this or that area ; with many abuses. Two early fourteenth-century examples of the latter may be noticed. In 1318 the King ordered the mayor and bailiffs of Chester to allow no civilians to enter with arms, as armed strangers had gone into the city on the day of the county court, some of them even being the keepers of the peace for the county, who, under colour of their office, went about armed and terrorized the people.[3] In 1327 the justiciar was ordered to summon the serjeants of the peace holding " in fee," and make them obedient to him in all that concerned their offices. If he found them negligent, their bailiwicks were to be taken into the King's hand, as the King heard that the serjeants had demised their offices, and that neither they nor their lessees executed their duties properly, and even concealed trespasses against the peace.[4]

---

[1] *Ib.*, 222 ; Ormerod, i, 356; Lysons, *Cheshire*, 571 ; *37 Rep. Dep. Keeper*, 376, etc.

[2] See my " The End of the Norman Earldom of Chester," *Eng. Hist. Rev.*, 35, 1920.

[3] *Cal. Pat. Rolls 1317-21*, p. 200. The reference to *custodes pacis* here is probably to the serjeants, as the *custos pacis* does not otherwise occur in Cheshire at this date.

[4] Appendix III, no. 20.

The system must have become all but ineffective by the end of the fourteenth century, during which century and the next Cheshire became, if not itself entirely a lawless county, a refuge for the criminals of its neighbours. Royal writs did not run there nor could the sheriff's officers of Shropshire or Staffordshire or those of the Marches enter the county. The parliamentary petitions and the statute roll amply illustrate these conditions. Then, too, the effect of the Black Death, like other visitations of the kind, was in part the encouragement of the evildoer and the riotous. We also find that the courts of the Hundreds, which had had so much to do with the initial steps of criminal justice, gradually became practically inoperative for want of vigorous application of their powers. The revenue from their jurisdiction, which had usually made it easy to let these courts to farm, fell away so much that it became hardly worth while to hold them [1]; and thus crime became unpresented and so unpenalized.

During the earldom of the Black Prince (1333–76), his Cheshire *Register* and the contemporary enrolments of his orders [2] seem to show that but little alteration or reform took place in the police system, though the forest laws were rigorously enforced and attempts were made to suppress crime by a threat of a " general eyre " (unknown in Cheshire), and by the actual holding of an equally severe commission of " trailbaston." [3] For some reason Sir John de St. Pierre was forced to surrender the county serjeanty of the peace, but he soon got it back again.[4] The Audley baronial serjeanty in Nantwich was indeed taken away for abuses, extortion and outrages on the community.[5] Peace recognizances were frequently resorted to at this date and the mayor and sheriffs of Chester were commanded to bind over offenders and thus to keep the peace there as well as it was (or should have been) kept in the county, the earl hearing that there were more criminals inside the city than out.[6] Here it is worth noting that in 1361 the mayor and commonalty of Chester successfully petitioned the earl that the justiciar or others of his officers should not interfere in regard to the

---

[1] *The Wapentake of Wirral*, 37, 62.

[2] *Black Prince's Reg.*, vol. iii (1932), relates entirely to Cheshire. The rolls referred to are the so-called Recognizance Rolls of Chester, calendared in the 36th, 37th and 39th *Reports of the Dep. Keeper of Pub. Records*.

[3] *Cal. Chester County Court Rolls*, xxx, and *Black Prince's Reg.*, iii, *passim*.

[4] *Black Prince's Reg.*, iii, 96–98.   [5] *Ib.*, iii, 138.

[6] *Ib.*, iii, 161.

labourers and craftsmen of the city but that the mayor and
sheriffs should deal with the judging and punishment of such
offenders.[1] This is a reference to the enforcement of the Statutes
of Labourers, a duty which was largely entrusted in the rest
of the kingdom to special justices of labourers or those of the
peace. As no such officials were yet at work in the county
palatine, the city authorities claimed jurisdiction by virtue of
their chartered rights while the enforcement of these statutes
elsewhere in the county was left as a rule in the hands of the
justiciar, though sometimes deputed to commissioners.[2]

Following upon a general proclamation of the peace in 1352
by the justiciar in full county court, the earl took the advice
of persons learned in the law who had been summoned to
Chester, and in 1353 caused certain ordinances for strengthening
the peace, the terms of which we are not told, to be reduced to
writing and proclaimed at the county court by the justiciar
twice and doubtless in the hundred courts as well. Moreover,
the earl becoming greatly angered and injured in his dignity
when he found his personal admonitions had been grievously
disregarded, publicly proclaimed the ordinances himself, in order
to give them more weight.[3] And so it must gradually have
become evident that the ancient system of preserving the peace
had broken down and that other methods must be found to
deal with the situation.

(i) THE COMMISSIONS *AD HOC*

The first reform adopted seems to have been that of issuing
special commissions *ad hoc* to trusted persons, authorizing and
ordering them to arrest malefactors and disturbers of the peace
within the counties of Chester and Flint, for it must be noted
that the latter had long been to all intents and purposes under
the palatine control. As early as 1359 a local commission
issued in connection with the general ordinances (based on the
statute of Winchester) made by the king for the safety of the
realm during his absence. By this writ the king directed the
prince to appoint by letters patent certain of the most considerable and trustworthy men of the county and principality to

---

[1] *Ib.*, iii, 415–16.
[2] In 1360, Kenard ap Roppert was appointed to inquire into infractions
in Flintshire of the laws regulating the wages of artificers and labourers
(*Cal. Chesh. Recog. Rolls, 36 Rep. Dep. Keeper*, Appendix II, p. 184).
In 1390 six commissioners were appointed to inquire into such infringe-
ments of these statutes (*ib.*, 181).
[3] *Black Prince's Reg.*, 77, 129.

carry out the array and arming of the countryside ; they were to have power to arrest all contrariants and rebellious, and were to erect the necessary beacons to warn all of the approach of any enemy.[1]

For the next twenty years or so the law everywhere seems to have relaxed its control over the maintenance of the peace, and the harsh and ineffective local government of the Black Prince reaped its reward in the disturbances which arose within the county throughout the troubled time of his son Richard, first as earl of Chester and then as king. To cope with the defiance of the law the special commissions to arrest were eventually revived. In 1365 the sheriff and four other magnates were given one to arrest the men of Lancashire crossing the Mersey at unauthorized places, while Warrington bridge was broken.[2] From 1386 many were issued. Six leading men of the Hundred of Northwich on 3 February 1385–86, two for that of Nantwich on the following 28 February, and three for Wirral on 28 May, were commissioned to deal with bands of armed men who were causing great terror and disturbances.[3] A commission in 1390[4] was for the seizure of the lawless concerned in the expulsion of a priest at Malpas ; by another, in 1391, the subsidy commissioners were given special powers to imprison all who had impeded the sheriff in the collection of the monies and taken part of it from him by force.[5] Commissions[6] both in January and April of 1392 to Sir Ralph de Vernon and others recite further serious riots, disturbances and breaches of the peace in the whole county. The offenders were to be seized and put in prison in the castle of Chester. In August of the same year two special commissioners for each of the seven hundreds were called for.[7] In 1394 and 1395[8] the sheriff had to be given extraordinary powers of arresting bold insurgents whose breaches of the peace had received no just punishment.

It seems clear that these commissions must be regarded as commissions " of the peace." For in 1396, for certain reasons not specifically mentioned, all letters patent and commissions, " lately " issued under the exchequer seal of Chester, to knights

---

[1] *Black Prince's Reg.*, iii, 377. No such letters seem to exist, either in the *Register* or on the Recognizance Rolls. A proclamation of 1362 forbade anyone to go armed, the prince hearing that bodies of men travelled the country committing felonies and trespasses in contempt of a former enactment made by the prince when last in Chester (*Cal. Recog. Rolls, 36 Report D.K.*, 93).

[2] *Cal. Chester Recog. Rolls, 36 Rep. D.K.*, 523. [3] *Ib.*, 53, 135, 189.
[4] *Ib.*, 131.   [5] *Ib.*, 96.   [6] Appendix III, no. 21.
[7] *Cal. ib.*, 160.   [8] *Ib.*, 97.

and esquires for keeping the peace and the arrest of evildoers, were to be recalled on public proclamation by the sheriff, for surrender at the exchequer after the next sitting of the county court.[1]

(j) THE CONSERVATORS OF THE PEACE

So far there has not been observed in Cheshire records any mention of the title or office of " conservator of the peace." [2] And, before going further, a reference may be noted to this office in the opinion,[3] given to the Queen in 1568, by four justices of the bench, on a question involving the jurisdiction of the county palatine and the authority of the chamberlain and his vice-chamberlain to arrest. It was asserted by these judges that the chamberlain of Chester, as chief of the local exchequer (the chancery), " was and time out of mind hath been a conservator of the peace by virtue of that office." This statement, adopted by Coke,[4] is difficult to support by record evidence but the chamberlain is found in the thirteenth century ordering the arrest of thieves, and also sitting on the bench with the justice of Chester, though apparently for the hearing of what would now be considered civil cases.[5] Although his real business was that of working head of the exchequer, he, as head of that tribunal and one of the judges, may be considered an *ex-officio* conservator of the peace. It was, moreover, his business to take and enroll the recognizances to keep the peace.

The title *conservator pacis*, identical here with *custos pacis*, first emerges clearly in the history of the county palatine when Henry of Lancaster entered Chester on 10 August 1399, just before the seizure of Richard II. The vivid account by Adam of Usk of the duke's march through Cheshire from Shrewsbury contains a passage illustrating the circumstances.[6] " The reasons why the duke decided to invade that country are, because, abetting the King as has been said, it ceased not to molest the realm for the space of two whole years with murders, adulteries, thefts, pillage and other unbearable wrongs ; and because it had risen up against the said duke and against his coming,

---

[1] Chester Recog. Roll 2/69, m. 11d. (12) (very illegible).
[2] The history of this office generally has been studied by Miss Putnam in numerous publications (*see* p. 141), and by Beard, *The Office of Justice of the Peace in England*. See also Professor Hazeltine's General Preface to Dowdell, *A Hundred Years of Quarter Sessions*.
[3] Ormerod, i, 128 ; *Cheshire Sheaf*, iii, vol. 23, p. 54; *Cheth. Soc.*, xxxvii, 32.
[4] *Fourth Inst.*, 212.   [5] *Cal. Chester County Court Rolls*, 18, etc.
[6] *Chronicon Adæ de Usk*, 2nd ed., 1904, pp. 26, 175.

threatening to destroy him. Another cause was on account of the right of exemption of that country wherein the inhabitants, however criminal elsewhere, and others entangled in debt or crime, were wont to be harboured as in a nest of wickedness, so that the whole realm cried vengeance upon them."

One of the first acts of the duke had been to depose and execute Scrope earl of Wiltshire, the justiciar of Chester and Flint, at Bristol on 30 July and when he reached Chester he made Henry Percy (Hotspur) justiciar, though the actual appointment was not enrolled until October,[1] after the deposition of Richard II, when a new staff of officials for the earldom of Chester, including a chamberlain, escheator, attorney-general and King's serjeants-at-law, superseded those of the previous regime.[2] The new justiciar at once issued, by authority of the council, letters patent,[3] entitled (inaccurately) in the heading as a *commissio custodum pacis* for the hundred of Edisbury. This document, to which Percy had to affix his own seal, not yet having possession of the late justiciar's seal of office, was dated 14 August 1399, Richard II having to be mentioned in it as still the king. It recited that Henry duke of Lancaster, *senescallus Anglie*, " had taken the community of Cheshire into his grace, and moreover, desiring peace and tranquility everywhere in the county to be inviolably kept, had appointed Sir Richard de Winnington and Richard Manley to be *conservatores pacis* in the Hundred of Edisbury." They were to make public proclamation in the duke's name in that hundred that no one of other counties or places was to seize the goods or chattels of those living in Edisbury against their will, and were to arrest all malefactors, rebels and peace disturbers found there, for imprisonment in the custody at Chester of the constable of the castle until sufficient security for good behaviour had been found. After this recital Percy's letters patent proceeded to announce that he had taken these conservators, their men, lands and possessions, into his protection (it doubtless remaining uncertain at the moment whether the men of Cheshire would continue loyal to the King or would turn, as they did, to welcome the future Henry IV). It seems unlikely that conservators were appointed for only one hundred, and it is fairly certain that the same course was then taken for all the other six but that these other appointments, not being strictly constitutional,[4]

---

[1] *Cal. Chester Recog. Rolls, 36 Rep. D.K.*, Appendix II, 100, 379.
[2] *Ib.*, 100, etc.   [3] Appendix III, no. 22.
[4] For a general survey of the constitutional aspects, see Lapsley, " The Parliamentary Title of Henry IV," *Eng. Hist. Review*, 50, 1935.

were not enrolled, our knowledge of the one for Edisbury being
due to its recital in a document issued for another object. An
appointment of 23 September 1399 of six conservators of the
peace for the hundred of Nantwich is regularly recorded on the
rolls as by Henry IV, though actually dated a week before his
accession.[1]

The next step, material to this account, after the creation
of Henry of Monmouth as earl of Chester in October 1399, was
a commission of 21 November by which a very large body of
" hereditary men and yeomen " of the hundred of Broxton were
made conservators of the peace, with special reference to robbers
from Shropshire and Flintshire who had taken refuge in that
hundred.[2] In January 1399-1400 another commission[3] of
keepers of the peace recites that large bodies of armed malefactors, both in the county and the city of Chester, continued
to roam about, collecting in illegal conventicles and meetings
and making proclamation in church, village, market and fair
that all defensible men must join them on pain of death and
mutilation, or waste of their homes. By reason of this and
other enormities dangerous to the whole of England which
contra pacem nostram clare resonant, the county was becoming
greatly perturbed and exhausted. Twelve or more joint and
several conservators were therefore commissioned by the new
earl for each of the seven hundreds, to seek out both past and
future rebels, and arrest and carry them to prison. All sheriffs,
mayors, bailiffs, officials and loyal men were to assist, but none
of these commissions refers to or includes the county serjeants
of the peace by name and their day was clearly over.

Many of these troubles had been due to the privileges of a
palatinate, and in 1384 the commonalties of the counties adjoining both those of Chester and Durham had complained to parliament that the inhabitants of these palatinates were accustomed
to make raids and commit crimes outside their borders. For
these, the petition declares, no punishment was appointed nor
was there any forfeiture of the goods and chattels of the Cheshire
men, by reason of their franchise.[4] Nothing, however, was then
done as regards either Cheshire or Durham, but in the first
year of Henry IV " grievous clamour and complaint " was
again renewed to the effect that residents in Cheshire com-

---

[1] *Cal. Chester Recog. Rolls, 36 Rep. D.K.*, Appendix II, 498.
[2] *Ib.*, p. 61. This shows that there had been an appointment by
Richard II of conservators for Broxton, as suggested above.
[3] Appendix III, no. 23.
[4] *Close Roll*, 1384, used by Lapsley, *Durham*, 227.

mitted felonies and trespasses in the neighbouring counties and, by escaping back into their own, evaded punishment by reason of the fact that process issued elsewhere could not be executed within the palatine limits. A remedy was provided by the statutory provision that process of outlawry issued in the county where the offence was committed could be certified to the officials of Cheshire and *vice versa*, and thus the felon and his goods were to be seized. The earl was to take such outlaws' forfeitures after enjoyment for a year and a day by the crown.[1] In the time of the Black Prince earlier attempts had been made to effect the same object by mutual extradition agreements (*kedivotes*) between him and the lords marchers for the surrender of criminals.[2]

In 1402, while the earl was absent in London and Owen Glendower was making trouble, a body of five " lieutenants " for the county of Chester and North Wales was appointed [3] for the general safeguard and good governance of those parts, and for the destruction of the rebels during the absence of the prince ; and it may be that in these officers, combining military duties with guardianship of public safety, can be seen the predecessors of the lords lieutenant first appointed in the time of Henry VIII. In that same year unprecedented enormities in the hundred of Macclesfield called for another commission of the peace there, and conservators were also appointed in the Maillor lordship of Flintshire.[4] In 1404 commissions were made in all the seven Cheshire hundreds.[5] Thus the conservators continued to function and in 1427 the coroners and bailiffs of all hundreds, the sheriff and the escheator, were included in a commission.[6]

In 1434, following a resolution of parliament, a commission was directed all over the country, intended to redress disturbance and miscarriages of justice, largely due to the protection given by the magnates to criminals who assumed their liveries. The chamberlain and vice-chamberlain of Chester, like the bishop of Durham, were amongst those who were directed to administer the necessary oath to the knights, esquires and men of substance

---

[1] Stat. I Henry IV, c. 18.
[2] *Black Prince's Reg.*, iii, 149, 490 ; cf. the methods in Durham, Lapsley, 226. These arrangements should be examined in detail.
[3] *Cal. Recog. Roll, 36 Rep. D.K.*, Appendix II, 101 ; also in 1403 (p. 102). There are many other orders referring to the Welsh rebellion which it is not necessary to mention here.
[4] *Ib.*, 313, 219, 337.   [5] *Ib.*, 103, 532.
[6] *Cal. Recog. Rolls, 37 Rep. D.K.*, 152–53.

of the county. This was to the effect that no lord or other person should wittingly receive, cherish, hold in his household or maintain " pilours," robbers, oppressors, manslayers, felons, outlaws, ravishers, unlawful forest hunters or other open or reputed misdoers, until their innocence had been proclaimed. Neither by feoffments nor gifts were such lords to take up others' quarrels, by favour, or maintenance, by word or writing, or by message to officials, judge, jury or party, or by giving of livery or taking into service such persons, nor create indignation or displeasure against any judge or official for doing his legal duty.[1]

The disturbances, which continued, required many further special commissions of conservators or of arrest which were issued in Cheshire all through the wars of the Roses. They occur in 1441, 1442, 1448, 1454, 1455, 1463, and 1481,[2] some being for Flintshire, and a commission in 1491[3] was to the mayor of Chester to arrest persons leaving the kingdom by ship, with the masters and owners. In 1435, 1442, 1445 and 1446 the master serjeant of the peace for Macclesfield Hundred, as such, was included in commissions[4] to arrest, which one would have supposed he would not ordinarily have required if his ancient powers still continued in force. These are the last occasions noted on which any of the medieval peace officers seem to have been officially employed and thereafter the hereditary offices of master serjeant must have become more or less titular in the families which held them.

The *quo warranto* inquiries of 1499[5] into the county franchises in Cheshire show that, although Lord Dudley, then the " baron " of Malpas, and representative of the hereditary county master serjeanty of the peace, claimed his " baronial " jurisdiction, he gave " no justification " for his claim to the county serjeanty (perhaps on account of sub-division of interests), and it seems to have disappeared. The master serjeanty of the peace in Macclesfield hundred was however formally claimed by Ralph Davenport and allowed[6]; and also the master forestership of Delamere. At this eyre of 1499 Sir William Stanley of Hooton

[1] *Ib.*, Appendix II, 135; *The Wapentake of Wirral*, 58; Lapsley, *Durham*, 227; and *Ancestor*, i, 57, where Sir G. Sitwell thought those to whom this oath was to be tendered were probably the supporters of the Yorkist cause.

[2] *37 Rep. D.K.*, 19, 184, 643, 644, 139, 101, 254, 805, etc.

[3] *Ib.*, 143.   [4] *Ib.*, 58, 121, 183, 184, 185.

[5] See my article in *Eng. Hist. Review*, Oct. 1934, and the details published in 1935 in the *Cheshire Sheaf*.

[6] See also *ante*, p. 11.

produced a relic of his ancestor's serjeanty in the forest of Wirral [1] by a claim that he or one of his serjeants could still represent his manor of Storeton at the hundred eyre at Backford by appearing there before the justiciar and sheriff with horn upraised, and after blowing a blast, could go away upon his business immediately, without more ado.

The officials summoned to this special " eyre " of 1499 included the *custodes pacis* of the county, by now a regular institution, but not yet with general commissions nor termed " justices of the peace."   Out of sixty claims to divers franchises, known to have been put forward at this date, upwards of twenty-five were for the jurisdiction mis-named " view of frankpledge." [2] Twelve of these also included the higher rights of jurisdiction covered by the words *infangthief* or *outfangthief*, gallows and the like.   Five of these twelve represented successors of the survivors of the original seven or eight " barons," and five others of them were monastic or ecclesiastical bodies which had obtained such rights.   But by this date the franchisal serjeants, like those of the county, had, as active peace officers, become obsolete, and they apparently survived only as bailiffs or bedells of the " barons' " courts, serjeants-at-mace and catch-polls of the " views of frankpledge," and rent collectors for their lords.   Cheshire was now to make a belated conformity with the rest of England by the establishment of the justices of the peace. [3]

---

[1] *Ante*, p. 12.
[2] Frankpledge proper was not in force in Cheshire (*post*, p. 99).
[3] See Appendix I.

CHAPTER II

THE SERJEANTS OF THE PEACE IN WALES

In the course of these investigations, a certain amount of evidence has been collected of the existence in Wales, in post-conquest times, of a system of serjeants of the peace. A thorough examination of the Welsh evidence must be left to others, but their labours may be slightly lightened if what has been gathered is here set out. The prevalence of the system is clearly shown, but a special study of all the Welsh sources would undoubtedly bring further information to light.

(a) The Serjeants of the Peace in Englefield

The dependence upon the rulers of Cheshire of the lands, now part of northern Flintshire, anciently known as Tegeingl or Englefield, stretches back to Domesday. In 1086 the district was part of the hundred of Atiscros, with a centre in the manor of Rhuddlan, and it was divided between the earl of Chester and his kinsman, Robert of Rhuddlan. Despite the loss of Englefield from time to time to the Welsh, the Norman earls of Chester continued to consider themselves entitled to collect its revenues when they could do so, and must have had both local courts and officers for this purpose. Any such organization as they had been able to set up and keep in operation passed to the crown with Cheshire in 1237, and it is in one of the early conciliatory acts of Henry III towards the Welsh that the first mention of the serjeants of the peace in this area seems to occur. On 5 May 1242, in a grant to the men of Englefield of various privileges, including acquittance of the food rents which they had formerly rendered to the princes of North Wales, it was provided that they were to be subject only to the jurisdiction of the royal court of Englefield and according to Welsh law and custom. They were to hold their lands of the King by a rent of £50 a year and by paying the cost of finding twenty-four serjeants of the peace.[1] How far this refer-

[1] Appendix III, no. 25. This charter was overlooked by Prof. Tout ("Flintshire," in *Flintshire Hist. Soc.*, 1911), J. G. Edwards (*Flint Pleas*, ib., 1922) and A. Jones (*Flint Min. Accts.*, ib., 1913).

ence indicates an earlier organization is not clear, but it seems extremely likely that the serjeants in this area were by no means a newly-imposed feature, though from time to time the district in which they functioned had to be evacuated under Welsh pressure. The charter of 1242 remained the authority under which the courts of Flintshire were conducted and doubtless for the obligation to maintain the serjeants there, long after the Statute of Wales (1284) had elevated the royal bailiff of Englefield into a county sheriff, and the charter was inspected and enrolled upon the Cheshire records as late as 1352.[1] A petition of the men of Englefield, undated but perhaps of the time of Edward II, asking for this charter to be confirmed, refers to their obligation to maintain the serjeants, which they said they had discharged, but they had recently been summoned to perform the serjeants' actual duties as well, contrary to the charter and to reason, for which they sought redress. The endorsed royal reply was that the justiciar of Cheshire was to lease out the serjeants' office under perpetual guarantee, certifying whether the rent or the profits were the more advantageous to the crown.[2]

The due payment of the fees for the maintenance of the serjeants of Englefield is recorded in the Flintshire receipts of the chamberlain of Chester from 1300 to 1326 [3] (and probably much later), where it is recorded that puture money of the serjeants, there called " porthyenkeys," was paid in semi-annually by the bedells of the three commotes of Tegeingl, viz. Coleshill ($£9$ 16s. 6d.), Prestatyn ($£9$) and Rhuddlan ($£7$ 15s.) with a small sum from the vill of Vaynol (in Rhos) which had been added to the new county of Flint in 1284.[4] The editor of these Flintshire accounts explains " porthyant cais " (as the scribe should have written these Welsh words) as the sustenance of the cais, glossed in the Latin of the accounts as potura serientis [pacis], and he regards cais as meaning " a seeker after " or " fetcher." [5] Evidently it was the Welsh for a serjeant of this kind.[6]

---

[1] Cal. Chesh. Recog. Roll, 36 Rep. D.K., 172.

[2] P.R.O. Anc. Petition 5462 (File 110), pr. in Cheshire Sheaf, iii, vol. 20, p. 88.

[3] Appendix III, no. 26 ; also, later, in A. Jones, Flint Min. Accts., 1913, and my Chesh. Chamberlains' Accts., 1910.

[4] J. G. Edwards, Flint Pleas 1283-85, 56. In these pleas William the serjeant (p. 5) and Eynion the serjeant (pp. 5 and 30) are mentioned.

[5] Jones, op. cit., xxvi, where ceisbwl, a catchpole, is noted. The editors of the Survey of Denbigh, 1334, also give the derivation of cais from caisiaw or keysyau, to seek, to fetch.

[6] See note, post, p. 46.

(b) Elsewhere in North Wales and the Marches

Though the serjeants of the peace have been found in the dependent district of Englefield immediately contiguous to Cheshire by 1242 and may have been there earlier, it seems unlikely that the system, if an innovation, can have been extended farther west into North Wales until the conquest by Edward I. The serjeants are not mentioned in the organizations set up by the Statute of Wales in 1284, though there were to be bailiffs in each of the commotes of Snowdon, but, as they existed already in the new Flintshire, they may well then have followed as officers under the justiciar of Snowdon with the coroners and sheriffs of the new counties of Anglesey, Caernarvon, and Merioneth, and in the lands of the marcher lords. There were already in the commotes, the administrative units under the ancient Welsh rule, officials of various kinds including mounted men, whose circuits (*cylch*) were maintained by exactions of food rents,[1] so that a system of police, maintained by similar methods, would be easily introduced, the more so if indeed the old Welsh organization had officers with somewhat similar functions, though they are not identifiable in the codes.

The collection of documents in the register known as the *Record of Caernarvon* includes a jumble of miscellaneous items, in Latin, under the title *Leges et Consuetudines Walliæ*. These begin with the Statute of Rhuddlan (1284) which is followed by an entry headed "the customs of Hereford," of no importance for this investigation. Then comes a number of items relating to the peace organizations, stated to have been contained *in recordis North Walliæ*, but all entirely undated. The explanation of the entry of these miscellaneous items, examined below, seems to lie in the history of the compilation of this so-called "Record" of Caernarvon. According to the editor's introduction, the bulk of the matter contained in the printed volume is taken from Harl. MS. 696 which represents a book ordered to be compiled in 1494, the MS. being "of that exact age" (another MS. used is of Elizabethan date). At the sessions held at Beaumaris on 22 May, 9 Henry VII (1494), an order was made by the justiciar and commissioners that the chamberlain of North Wales, the sheriff, the escheator, and all other

---

[1] See the codes of Welsh laws ; the charter, dated 1198, of Llewellyn, prince of North Wales, to the monks of Aberconway, gave them acquittance from *pastus* and *puture* of men, horses, dogs and birds and from feeding him or his officers or other secular persons by way of custom (*Cal. Charter Roll*, iv, 267).

officers who made out any process for the prince, were to enter these, and all other things belonging to their office, in a book, and at the end of the year make " a substance " of the same book, to be entered in parchment and lodged in the Exchequer of Caernarvon, as of old time accustomed, there to remain " of record." Likewise, the clerk of the sessions was to make entry " of record " of all things concerning felonies, or breaches of the peace, and these entries were also to be sent into the Exchequer and to remain " of record." [1] On this basis the successive items stated to have been found *in recordis* seem to represent notes entered up by the sessions clerk of matters concerning felonies and breaches of the peace, pursuant to the order of 1494.[2] The records from which they were extracted have presumably perished.[3]

Returning to the extracts, after a preliminary note that by the Statute of Rhuddlan (1284) the justice of North Wales (sometimes called of Snowdon) had the keeping and governance of the King's peace there and in the adjacent Welsh lands, and that the laws of England, not Wales, were to apply to felonies and other matters, there then comes the first of three curious and undated statements referring to the serjeants of the peace.[4]

The first is stated to have been found *inter ordinacionem pro pace in North Wallia*. It is to the effect that, at the instance and request of the community of the county of Merioneth, the justice had ordered and publicly proclaimed that the conservators of the peace called " keys " (*cais*) were abolished. If any felony took place in that county, with hue raised and prosecuted, the whole county would answer for the felons' bodies, the stolen goods and satisfaction of the robbery. The community under-

---

[1] *Rec. of Caernarvon*, Introduc., first para., and p. 295.

[2] Vinogradoff, *Growth of the Manor*, 8, states that the *Record of Caernarvon* was drawn up in 1354 but does not show how that date is arrived at.

[3] As the volume contains some instructions as to the methods of certifying extracts from records, one would have expected it to give, by references, some means of finding them. But the clerk doubtless knew where they were and performed his duty perfunctorily.

[4] Appendix III, no. 27. The editor of the *Flint Min. Accts.*, pp. xxvi–vii, appears to think the statements in the *Record of Caernarvon* come from the " Statute of Wales " where, he says, we read them (p. xxvi), and he writes of that statute as explaining the meaning of *cais*, and as abolishing the office (p. xxvii). Nothing of the kind is, of course, in the statute. Nor was the office peculiar to North Wales (p. xxvii), as this essay abundantly shows. In a review of the *Flint Min. Accts.* in the *Chester Chronicle* about June 1913, Professor (Sir) J. E. Lloyd asked, " What was the *cais* whose *porthiant* or ' support ' is a prominent feature in these accounts ? " and agreed that he was not the *canghellor*, as suggested by Palmer and Owen.

took under penalty both to do this and to observe the lord's peace. The same took effect in other counties (not named).

The next following item is that, according to the ancient law of Wales in North Wales, there were conservators of the peace called " keys " in all counties, for whom the whole country (*patria*) was bound by the laws of Wales to find sustenance (*victus*), and in return the " keys " guarded the country from malefactors and answered for their bodies and their deeds. Because the whole country had felt itself greatly burdened with finding the *potura* and sustenance of the " keys," they had been abolished at the petition of the community, which in return gave an undertaking for the observation of the peace everywhere in North Wales and to answer for felonies, thefts and the bodies of malefactors.

The third item (which does not follow immediately) states that it was found in divers records that because many homicides and robberies by malefactors and disturbers of the peace had taken place in many places within the county of Caernarvon, whereof complaints had frequently been made to the justice by those aggrieved, the justice, for the preservation of the peace, made to come before him all the better and more honest Welshmen of the county having full power for the community of the whole county, to make ordinance and to enact together, with advice of the justice, a fit remedy upon the premises ; and they, by ordinance made between the justice and themselves, undertook for themselves and the whole community of the county to preserve the peace of the king in the same county and ordained keepers of the peace (*ordinaverunt custodes pacis*) in each commote, and for themselves undertook that no thieves, homicides or breakers of the king's peace, persons indicted, outlawed or notorious inhabitants or foreigners, should be received. When such came to their notice, they would arrest them or answer for their misdeeds. And afterwards the said community, for divers murders not presented and adjudged upon the community, and for not preserving the peace according to the ancient ordinance, and for concealment of presenting defaults of free tenants who did not come before the justice on the first day of his eyre, was fined . . . ccccv marks, and was charged as formerly with keeping the peace according to the ordinance, etc. [*sic*.]. The Welsh community of the county of Merioneth for the same cause was amerced as much and charged with keeping the peace as before, etc. [*sic*.]. The Welsh community of the county of Anglesey in like wise.

The first statement quoted above indicates that there were in North Wales conservators of the peace called " keys " (cais) ; and that they had been abolished both in Merioneth and some other counties by public proclamation, of unknown date, by the justice; the second statement also records the abolition of the cais, and adds that the whole country in North Wales had been responsible for their sustenance. According to both these two statements, the counties, or country, had undertaken themselves to be responsible in future for the acts, deeds, and bodies of felons and the results thereof ; though how this was carried out is not explained.

The third statement shows that agreements [1] had been made with the justice by the men of the counties of Caernarvon, Merioneth and Anglesey to be responsible for the peace and that they appointed their own custodes pacis in each commote, under undertakings by the communities to keep out evildoers. At a later date, for breaches of the " ancient ordinance " for the preservation of the peace and other defaults, the communities of each of the three counties were heavily fined and charged with their former obligations according to the " ancient ordinance." This " ancient ordinance " of the peace for North Wales has not been discovered. It is possible that it was based upon the Statute of Winchester (1285) which was directed against the neglect of the community in England to report robbery, murder and felonies, and required fresh suit to be made against offenders and inquests to be held in towns, franchises, hundred and county. The statute also provided that if a county would not answer for the bodies of offenders, the people of the whole hundred where the crime was committed were to be answerable for all felonies, robberies and damages. The justice of Snowdon may have issued a special ordinance under this statute, or under the powers given to him as custos pacis by the Statute of Wales.

The wording of the statements referred to may be open to other interpretations, but it is suggested that they mean that the abolition of the serjeants, whenever that occurred, was subsequently revoked. This view is supported by the evidence given below that it was not until the first decade of the sixteenth century that the serjeant's puture, under various names, was abolished, by three separate charters, for the counties of Merioneth, Caernarvon, and Anglesey, for Chirkland, and for

---

[1] Mr. Waters appears to place the date of these arrangements as about 1301 (Edwardian Settlement of North Wales, 29-30).

the lordship of Bromfield and Yale. The burden of payment
of this puture had been the grounds upon which the serjeants
had previously been abolished and from the continuance of this
obligation in some of these areas in the early sixteenth century
the existence of the serjeants also may perhaps be inferred.
On the other hand there is no mention of the *cais* or the collection of his maintenance in the survey and rental of Merioneth
dated about 1292,[1] or in the earliest extant account of the
sheriff of Caernarvon for 1303–04,[2] or in that of the chamberlain
of North Wales for the following year.[3] The matter must be
left for elucidation.

The following undated petition evidently shortly followed
the abolition of the *cais*, whenever that occurred, and is additional
evidence that the step had not been successful. It was addressed
to the master steward of Chirkland by the royal tenants of
Kennleth and Mochnant there, and alleged that daily robberies
and thefts took place, the thieves escaping into Powysland,
Mawddwy, Merionethshire and the adjoining counties, " all in
defaute of a good officer for keepyng of the countrey, as hath
been accustomed in tymes paste. For the sergeaunt of peas
callyd the pencayse [master serjeant] hathe used to watch in
dyvers places . . . and take thevis and mysrewlye persons and
bring thame to the castell, wiche watche and excercise of the
said office made odre outlaws and theves for fere of the same to
forbere and durst not invade ne cume within the said countreis,
tyll this ij yeres paste that that office hath not been delygently
exercised ne occupiede, to the great inpoveryshenge and undoying
of all the trewman in the said countreis and the incresyng of
thevis and evyll rewlyd persons." The steward was begged to
authorize the appointment in such countries of a " cayse " for
the love of God and the administration of justice.[4] The *cais*
in this area is mentioned below.

In the introduction to the *Survey of the Honour of Denbigh
1334*,[5] in which survey occur items for the annual value of the
office of the serjeant of the peace and his " satellites " in the

---

[1] P.R.O. Surveys and Rentals 789 (*Arch. Cambrensis*, iii, vol. 12).
I owe this reference to Mr. T. P. Ellis.

[2] *Bulletin Board of Celtic Studies*, vii, 143.

[3] *Ib.*, i, 256. Mr. Waters, in his analysis of the revenues for Caernarvon,
Anglesey and Merioneth 1291–1340 does not mention any items of the
kind (*Edwardian Settlement of North Wales*, Appendixes VII, VIII, IX).

[4] Mahler, *Chirk Castle and Chirkland*, 114, from Brit. Mus. Stow MS.,
141, f. 34.

[5] Ed. Vinogradoff and Morgan, 1914 (vol. i, *Records of Social and
Economic Hist. of Eng. and Wales*), lxxxiii *sqq.*

commote of Cymeirch, the two commotes of the cantred of
Rhufoniog, and the two of that of Rhos,[1] the editors (Professor
Vinogradoff and Mr. Morgan) regard the serjeant definitely as
an importation from the English system. They point out that
in the old Welsh laws the preservation of the peace seems to
have rested upon a system of information and compurgation,
punishable by fines, but by what means felons were arrested
and imprisoned is not clear. The *canghellor*, with whom some
had identified the *cais*, had no powers of criminal jurisdiction
or imprisonment. "The English system of having regular
officers of justice appointed to pursue and detain felons spread
everywhere in Wales." The writers then refer to the second
statement quoted above [2] from the *Record of Caernarvon*, and
point out that, though it is there asserted that the office of
cais rested upon the old Welsh law, it is not mentioned, nor
is such an official even hinted at, in such codes as we have.
After referring to the payment in the fourteenth century in
the commotes of Englefield of the *porthyant cais* which has been
already mentioned, these writers point out that in other marcher
lordships the office seems to have fallen gradually into abeyance,
though the payment exacted for the serjeant's *cylch* was continued in the lordships of Yale and Bromfield until the first
decade of the sixteenth century.[3]

The most recent reference to this subject is that made by
Mr. Waters when discussing the administration of justice in
criminal matters after the conquest of North Wales.[4] He adopts
the view that before that date Wales had strictly no criminal
justice, serious offences being regarded as derogatory not so
much to the state as to the kindred. By the Statute of Wales
the old Welsh law was abrogated as regards serious crime which
was to be governed by the law of England. The statute also
introduced the hue and cry and threw the duty to pursue the
criminal upon the townships. Its provisions were seemingly
reinforced by the application in Wales of the police regulations
of the Statute of Winchester, commotal responsibility being
preferred to the former system. "Before the conquest officers
known as *keys* maintained the peace of the country but they
had to be supported by food-renders. This was burdensome
to the community and the demand for its abolition by the

---

[1] Appendix III, no. 28.   [2] *Ante*, p. 37.
[3] This seems to be a reference to Palmer and Owen, *Anc. Tenures
of Land in North Wales*, 2nd ed., p. 195, etc., mentioned below.
[4] *The Edwardian Settlement of North Wales in its Administrative and
Legal Aspects*, 1935, pp. 134–39.

native Welsh was granted on condition that the separate commotes should answer for the bodies of felons and make satisfaction for any robberies committed." Mr. Waters quotes no
authority for the ancient existence of the *cais* and his statement
seems inconsistent with the view which he expresses as to the
absence of criminal justice. He reads the entries in the *Record
of Caernarvon* as pointing to drastic measures adopted by the
justice of North Wales for the establishment and preservation
of peace and order and as suggesting, on the one hand, a return
to " the old system " of keepers of the peace and, on the other,
the enforcement of communal responsibility for crime. The
cais is not further considered in this book which deals mainly
with administrative conditions in Anglesey, Caernarvon and
Merioneth and hardly touches the eastern marcher lordships of
North Wales.

In the Extent, made in 1315, of the eastern marcher lordship
of Bromfield and Yale, then in the hands of the earl of Warrenne
and Surrey under the crown, there are only two references to
the maintenance of the serjeants. In Llarnarmon, a holder of
land of inheritance and also of one acre of demesne is recorded
as formerly having paid 2s. 1d. for the " potura " of divers
bailiffs in addition to his rents, which had been increased, and
he was to be quit for life of all maintenance of bailiffs on the
basis that his inherited land was then to pass to the earl. In
Dutton Diffaeth a *nativus* with a small holding provided puture
for the bailiffs guarding the peace or eighteenpence a year.[1]
The editor of this Extent comments on the absence of references
to *kylch* (puture) and on the fact that these are the only two
mentions of the serjeant's maintenance. This, he considers,
shows that there had, at this date, been no determined effort
to introduce in this area an impost for the entertainment of
the serjeants of the peace, " an officer introduced by the
Normans," which had met with vigorous opposition and repudia-
tion elsewhere as a new levy opposed to Welsh custom, though
many holders of land had been willing to provide puture if it
was not claimed as a matter of right.[2]

It is clear, however, that whatever was done in Merioneth
and other western counties, the system existed and had not
been abolished in the lordship of Bromfield and Yale by the
end of the fourteenth century and later, for in 1398 we find

[1] *Extent of Bromfield and Yale, 1315*, ed. T. P. Ellis (Soc. of Cymmrodorion, Rec. Ser. xi, 1924), pp. 83, 98.
[2] *Ib.*, 28-29.

two appointments to the office of serjeant of the peace. By the first John Hope was granted for life that office in the raglory, courts and bailiwicks of Wrexham and Marford, the two commotes of Bromfield, and the same office in Yale. It is there called the office of *pensitheth* [1] (*rectius* " pen-cais-iaeth," *i.e.* master serjeanty of the peace). By the second order John Sy was appointed serjeant of the peace in Yale for life, and the office is mentioned there in 1467 and later.[2]

There is evidence of the system in the lordship of Chirkland during the fourteenth and fifteenth centuries. Among the revenues in 1332 70s. is shown *pro potura satellitum*,[3] and the extent of 1391–93 includes *cylch cais* among the dues payable in Mochnant, though no amounts are entered.[4] At this date the office of *cais* was held with that of *ringild* (*ringild et seith*). The composite officer is described as appointed by the lord to collect the issues, rents, farms and debts, and to carry out arrests and executions pertaining to the offices of bailiff and coroner. His fees included a proportion of the amercements and fines, 6d. as *cylch* from each dwelling of villein tenants, 4d. from those of tenants on demesne lands, 1d. a year from occupiers of free tenements and free tenants without under-tenants, 4d. for stray animals taken into custody, and perquisites from the goods of felons, fugitives and intestates forfeited to the lord.[5] The editor of this Extent considers the *cais* as probably originally distinct from the *ringild* and seems inclined to accept the view that the former was an English importation, though he suggests that the *rhingyll* of the ancient laws of Wales may have developed into a peace officer.[6] The *exploratores* of the *cais* in Chirkland are mentioned in 1399 and an appointment to the office there was made in 1496,[7] the " kays " also being mentioned in 1498.[8]

This leads up to the three important royal charters of liberties already mentioned, to the men of Bromfield and Yale, to those of Chirkland, and to the inhabitants of Anglesey, Caernarvon and Merioneth. The charters are of successive years of Henry VII and all much to the same effect in regard to the *cais*, though

[1] *Chesh. Recog. Roll, 36 Rep. Dep. Keeper*, Appendix II, 2 and 5.
[2] *Ib.*, 462. In 1467 the officers of the lordship of Bromfield and Yale included the serjeant of the peace (Palmer, " The Town of Holt," *Arch. Camb.*, 1906–10).
[3] *The Extent of Chirkland 1391–93*, ed. G. P. Jones, 1933, p. 90.
[4] *Ib.*, 62–3–4, 66, etc.   [5] *Ib.*, 5.   [6] *Ib.*, pp. xxx-xxxii.
[7] Palmer and Owen, *op. cit.*, 197–98. The Acts of Resumption of 1464, 1485 and 1495 reserved the rights of the serjeants of the peace in the lordship of Denbigh (*Rot. Parl.*, v, 541b, vi, 380b, 466a).
[8] *Powys Fadog*, iv, 37, 38.

otherwise varying. That of 8 August 1505 for Bromfield and Yale [1] was addressed to the king's tenants and inhabitants of the lordship and, besides revoking for them the prohibition by act of Henry IV (1400) against Welshmen holding land or becoming a burgess, sheriff, mayor or *custos* of the peace in England or in English boroughs in Wales, and also purporting to abolish gavelkind, the charter excused them for ever from serving the offices of *raglot* or *ringild*, and abolished (with several other customary exactions) [2] the " farm " of the serjeant of the peace called *cylch kais* (*firma serjiantis pacis aliter vocata cylch kais* [3]), as well as the issues of the office of *raglot* and *ringild*, namely oats and litter for the horse and a penny as fee (*kylgh*), none of which moneys was to be collected in future. The charter for Chirkland, of 20 July 1506,[4] gave very similar privileges and likewise abolished the *kylch kais* and *kylch ringild*. Then followed the grant, dated 3 March 1507, to the inhabitants of Anglesey, Caernarvon and Merioneth,[5] again much to the same effect, the exactions abrogated here including the *pastus pennakays*, the maintenance of the *pen-cais* (the master serjeanty of the peace). From this date therefore the old system seems to disappear in these areas, though none of these charters in terms abolished the office itself, which may have continued under a salary as opposed to the puture system.[6] No evidence has been noticed that the serjeants of Flintshire or their puture money were ever definitely abolished and they may have died the lingering death which fell to those of Cheshire itself.

The special commission of arrest had been employed in several of these Welsh areas as well as in Cheshire.[7] In Flintshire in

---

[1] *Cal. Pat. Roll 1494–1509*, p. 434 ; A. N. Palmer brought these charters to light but did not know of the enrolments. He gives a poor version in his *Anc. Tenures in North Wales*, 1st ed., 127, and in "Two Charters of Henry VII " (*Y Cymmrodor*, xix). Palmer and Owen, *Anc. Tenures in North Wales*, 2nd ed., 173, state this charter was held to be invalid, so far as the abolition of gavelkind was concerned, though probably valid otherwise ; the change was made later by statute. See *Extent of Chirkland*, p. xv.

[2] See Palmer and Owen, *Anc. Tenures of Land in N. Wales*, 191 *sqq.*

[3] *Cylch* became *kelk* in Cheshire, a name for puture (Ormerod, iii, 64 n.).

[4] *Cal. Pat. Roll cit.*, 464 ; poor version by Palmer, " Two Charters of Henry VII," and Mahler, *Chirk Castle*, 109.

[5] *Cal. Pat. Roll cit.*, 534. The charter is not there printed but a reference made to *Archæologia Cambrensis*, ii (1847), 215–22, where it is printed in full. Henry VIII inspected and confirmed, *ib.*, ii, 292 ; *Powys Fadog*, i, 395.

[6] From 1505 to 1519 a serjeant " of the country " occurs among the officers in Bromfield and Yale. He was a paid official, with £4 a year (Palmer, " The Town of Holt," *loc. cit.*).

[7] For the latter, see *ante*, p. 25.

1394 the escheator of Flint and the coroner of Englefield were joined with others in a commission to inquire into unwonted robberies ; and the deputy sheriff and the coroner in others of 1441 and 1442,[1] while in 1360 a special commissioner had been appointed to inquire into breaches of the Statute of Labourers, duties which in England fell to the justices of labourers or of the peace. In Hopedale and in the commotes of Prestatyn and Coleshill, commissions of persons to keep watches against the activities of Owen Glendower issued in 1403.[2] An important commission to arrest disturbers of the peace in the Marches and the lordship of Bromfield and Yale occurred in 1428,[3] and doubtless there were others in these districts closely attached to Cheshire. Only one appointment of conservators of the peace in such areas has been noticed, namely for English Maelor in 1402,[4] but this makes it clear that the same special measures to preserve the peace were adopted here as in the county palatine.[5] In the next century Wales, like Cheshire, was to fall into line with England in the appointment of the justices of the peace.[6]

(c) South Wales

The existence of the serjeants in South Wales and its Marches has been demonstrated in the researches of Professor William Rees into the social and agrarian conditions in these areas in medieval times,[7] and the evidence which follows is taken almost entirely from his study. The serjeants are to be found in the Welshries, and in certain Englishries, of Cardigan, Carmarthen, Pembroke, Radnor, Glamorgan, Monmouth,[8] and Brecon, and in lordships in several parts of Herefordshire.[9] The organizations included in some places a master serjeant (*pencais*) with his satellites (*ceisiaid* or *keysettry*), and the names used for the officers or office were *servientes pacis, cais* or *keys* and *teulu*

---

[1] *Cal. Chesh. Recog. Roll, 36 Report D.K.,* 219, *37 Report,* 367.
[2] *Ib., 36 Report,* 247, 261, 392.   [3] *Ib., 37 Report,* 378.
[4] *Ib., 36 Report,* 219, 337.
[5] Though Anglesey and Caernarvon are often mentioned in the *Chesh. Recog. Rolls,* no commissions, either of arrest or of conservators of the peace, for such counties occur there.
[6] See Appendix II.
[7] *South Wales and the March, 1284–1415,* 1914.
[8] To the evidence for Monmouthshire may be added a charter of Walter de Lacy (d. 1241) to the priory of Llanthony, giving acquittance from compulsory feeding of any steward, constable, bailiff, *keys,* or forest serjeant. Appendix III, no. 29.
[9] In 1198 there was a serjeanty here for making summonses and bearing the royal treasure (*Book of Fees,* i, 6), but this may have been an office of a different type from those noted by Mr. Rees.

(a band). The serjeants, here serving under the beadle or *rhingyll*, acted as the police of the district, arresting evildoers of every description, distraining debtors and carrying into effect the decisions of the courts, including the hanging of felons. The community provided them with food and lodging (*cylch cais*) or the equivalent of a penny a day for each officer. In some areas a lump sum was paid for freedom from the maintenance of the English and Welsh serjeants. The numbers of officers varied. Two for each unit was usual for Welshries of the March, while in the commotes there was generally one for each *gwestfa* as the units from which the dues were payable came to be termed. The office was sometimes farmed, though there was often difficulty in finding lessees. In certain areas Mr. Rees thinks that the lords abolished the serjeants, but retained the dues which continued to be payable for a long period under the names of *serjeantsilver*, *silver of keys* or *boiteulu*.

Mr. Rees apparently rejects the view that the office of *cais* had an English origin, as he considers that it clearly dates from the Welsh regime and at latest from the eleventh century, on the grounds that he found that many Welsh districts of the March still contributed to the serjeants, as did isolated Welsh groups in Englishries and even individuals, in contrast to their English neighbours ; and he considered that before 1282 [? 1284] the office of *serviens pacis* was well established in the southern half of the Principality.[1] This view does not seem to take into account the possibility that it was after the twelfth-century English colonizations in South Wales and the conquests of the Marcher lords, that the serjeants were introduced. The Welsh communities would be likely to be saddled with their maintenance and the obligation in both North and South Wales seems to have been imposed wholesale and not upon a tenurial basis as in Cheshire and Lancashire. It lay upon the Welsh community in general, and though this is not incompatible with a Welsh origin, it looks more like an imposition upon a conquered race than an ancient customary obligation. Exempted areas, such as there were elsewhere, do not seem to occur here, though there were places in South Wales where the obligation appears to have been redeemed at dates since the conquest of Wales. That the serjeants were established in South Wales before the statute of 1284 may perhaps be explained by its earlier conquest and colonization by Englishmen. Mr. Rees does not comment upon the fact that the Welsh codes do not refer to these officers,

[1] Rees, *op. cit.*, 103–07.

but elsewhere in his book expresses the view that the laws are not comprehensive, being silent on many important matters, and do not necessarily record the common law of Wales in all its details as practised on the eve of the conquest.[1] He regards the Statute of Wales as having introduced into the crown lands in these areas the principle of the complete responsibility of each commote for all crime committed within its limits and thus, in addition to an earlier obligation to maintain the keepers of the peace, the community had imposed upon it the further burden of producing the body of the criminal or suffering heavy amercement. He finds that in certain areas of the March the duty of arrest, and of guarding prisoners and claimants of sanctuary, was an obligation both of individuals and communities which was occasionally abrogated by charter.[2]

NOTE ON THE WELSH *CAIS*

Professor Ifor Williams, Professor of the Welsh Language and Literature at the University College of North Wales, who was good enough to consider whether the literary history of the Welsh word *cais* threw any light upon the antiquity of the Welsh office of serjeant of the peace, points out that the absence of any all-Welsh MSS. dating earlier than about 1200 makes it impossible to say more than that *cais, ceis, kais,* is an early Welsh word, meaning " a search," " a quest." It is so used in the romantic tale " Breuddwyd Rhonabwy," where men were sent to seek for Jorwarth Madog ; *Agwr aoed ar y keis hwnnw sef oed y enw Ronabwy* (" and there was a man called Ronabwy who was upon that quest ") (*Mabinogion*, ed. Guest (1869) ii, 372) ; also in *Y Seint Greal* (the Welsh version of the Quest for the Holy Grail) where the quest is called *keis* and the knights who took part in it *keissyiet (ceisiaid).* From the word *cais, ceis,* comes the verb *keysyau, ceisiaw,* " to seek " " to fetch," which is used in one of the earliest Welsh MS. of *c.* 1200 (Lewis, *Glossary of Mediæval Welsh Law,* 70). In Welsh literary texts *cais* is thus used as an abstract noun = " the search " ; and " the seeker " would therefore be *ceisiad* (plural *ceisiaid*), which Professor Williams considers would be a natural name to be given to an English official introduced to hunt for wrongdoers. *Ceisiaid* occurs above in the South Wales evidence, p. 44, but in North Wales *cais* seems to be used for both the official and the office. The same with *pen cais,* as the head of the band of searchers. Professor Williams notes that Loth, *Les Mots Latins dans les Langues Brittoniques,* 1892, gives *ceis,* recherche, enquête, = *cestio, quæstio* ; and *ceis,* dans les lois a le sens de *custos pacis* (Wotton, *Gloss*), but considers the borrowing is not certain, comparing the Irish *ceis,* a circuit, visit. Irish *ceist* Loth derives from the Latin, though from *quæstio* one would expect *kweist* (cf. Pedersen, *Vergleichende Grammatik,* 1909–11, i, 213).

[1] Rees, *op. cit.,* 2–3   [2] *Ib.,* 59, 62.

CHAPTER III

THE SERJEANTS IN THE NORTHERN AREAS

In this chapter some of the records of Lancashire, Cumberland, Westmorland, Durham and Northumberland, areas which had comprised the old Kingdom of Northumbria, will be examined in turn for references to the serjeants.

Though the entries in Domesday Book for " Between Ribble and Mersey " (which is the only part of the northern counties for which details are given) do not mention the serjeants of the peace, there are several statements suggestive of the existence of such officers and pointing to a likely field for their activities in the detection of the reserved royal pleas of theft, breach of the peace, bloodshed and rape. For such offences, for absence from the shiremote without excuse, non-attendance at a plea when summoned by the reeve, and refusal to go on the latter's service, fines were payable to the king in the thegnages and drengages unless the holder of the manor had himself the right to take such forfeitures.[1] It is, however, for lack of evidence not until much later that the peace officers can actually be shown at work in these districts. But they are then found in such environment as supports an inference of their antiquity. For, as is well known, it is in these northern counties that the serjeants occur, in post-conquest times, in close association with the thegn and the dreng. Dr. Reid, when demonstrating that tenure by " barony " and thegnage implied an office to which were attached rights of public jurisdiction,[2] in her investigation of the status of the Anglo-Saxon thegn, found the king's thegn as a royal official with delegated (hundredal) judicial and administrative rights and duties akin to those of the sheriff, and with a general police jurisdiction over breach of the peace, manslaughter and bloodshed, including the right to execute the hand-having thief taken within his jurisdictional area. It was in the courts of such privileged persons that charges made against those in their *borh*, as well

[1] *V.C.H., Lancs.*, i, 285 *sqq.*
[2] " Barony and Thanage " (*Eng. Hist. Rev.*, 35, 1920).

47

as against the latter's pledgees, fell to be heard. Much of the evidence used by Miss Reid comes from these Northumbrian districts, and some of it is material to the purpose of this investigation. The cornage tenants in the baronies of Cumberland and Westmorland, who are identified as drengs, distinguishable only from thegns by duties of personal service, paid " serjeants' food " or puture as one of their customary dues, as well as cornage and other renders, the " baron " accounting for the latter to the exchequer but retaining the puture for the maintenance of his own serjeants. The puture payable outside these baronies was collected by the sheriff for the maintenance of the royal serjeants of the peace. Miss Reid also used for her purpose some of the Lancashire evidence given below demonstrating the jurisdictional rights of the " barons " holding there under Roger of Poitou, whose successors' privileges included the maintenance of a *grith* serjeant to keep the peace and the obligations of " bode " and " witness." The existence of the two sets of officers, royal and baronial, which will be still further demonstrated in detail below, was made clear.

Dr. Farrer has suggested,[1] with some confidence, that the survival into the reigns of Richard I and John of these drengages and thegnages points to the presumption that the greater number of the manors so held had descended in unbroken possession to their owners from pre-conquest forefathers, a conclusion which accords with the general impression of antiquity suggested by a system of serjeants of the peace maintained by the contributions of these holdings.

(1) LANCASHIRE

There are abundant records which show that the system existed in Lancashire. No attempt has been made to trace the decline of the Lancashire serjeants nor, for the reasons indicated on an earlier page,[2] the institution in this area of the keepers or the justices of the peace. Both of these appeared in Lancashire, as well as in the other areas dealt with below, considerably earlier than in Cheshire, and the serjeants' importance and duties must have been similarly affected by the independent action of the keepers and by the direction to the justices of writs and orders which had formerly been executed by the sheriff and the serjeants.

The Lancashire material throws light upon the Cheshire system and comes mainly from records of the late twelfth, the

---

[1] *V. C. H., Lancs.*, i, 283.　　　[2] *Ante*, p. xi.

thirteenth and the fourteenth centuries, when the system is seen in working order. There is an absence of evidence during the difficult feudal history of Lancashire between Domesday and the middle of the twelfth century, but before the date (1194) when royal overlordship was clearly re-established and the baronial jurisdictions plainly defined, the serjeants are clearly seen at work.

The general features of the Lancashire and Cheshire systems are very similar, though the terminology is often different and in Lancashire suggestive of greater antiquity. The main differences doubtless arose out of the slow welding of Lancashire into a county. Thus, while in Cheshire there was a master serjeant of the peace for the county, in Lancashire there was a royal serjeant for each of the hundreds. In Cheshire the baronial areas were not formed by grants of a hundred, but in Lancashire this was often the case with the greater baronies, and so, while the king's hundred serjeant functioned there for the performance of all royal duties attached to his office, and as *custos pacis* in respect of pleas of the Crown within each hundred, the serjeants of the " barons " and lords acted for all other purposes both as the peace officers of the sheriff in respect of the limited jurisdiction of the hundreds, and of their lords, as owners of delegated jurisdictional powers. In this way the hundred courts and those of the greater " barons " became almost indistinguishable and their identities obscured. So while in the Cheshire system we see three regular sets of peace officers, those of the county, of one of the hundreds, and of the " barons," in Lancashire we generally see but two, the royal serjeants of the hundreds and those of the " barons " as lords of the hundreds or of smaller units. The existence of a *grith* serjeant elected by the men of the hundred of West Derby is demonstrated, and affords a parallel for the suggestion made above that the bedells of the Cheshire hundreds were similarly chosen. The elective serjeant in Lancashire seems to have disappeared in the thirteenth century during the difficulties caused by the de Ferrers regime in the southern hundreds.

Some confusion which has been made between the royal and the baronial officers in Lancashire,[1] has been pointed out,[2] but the reason for the existence side by side of the different sets of officers in the hundreds of Lancashire has not been driven

[1] In the *V.C.H.*, *Lancs.*
[2] By Porteus in *The Hundred of Leyland*, Cheth. Soc., N.S., 90, 12–23, 63 *sqq.*

E

home. It lies in reserved royal, and delegated limited, juris-diction respectively, and is better seen in the more highly developed, if not hundredal, organizations in the county of Chester. The differences in terminology alluded to are the use in Lancashire and some other areas of the antique-sounding title of *grith* or peace serjeant, and the compendious description of his privileges as those of *serjeant's fode* (sometimes *fold*),[1] *bode and witnessmen*.[2] Some notes on the latter, and on the title of *grith* serjeant, are given below.

(a) THE HUNDRED OF WEST DERBY

The master serjeanty of this hundred (which absorbed the Domesday hundreds of Warrington and Newton) was granted,[3] apparently between 1157 and 1159, to Waldeve de Walton and his heirs by William earl Warenne, only surviving son of King Stephen, to whom the honour of Lancaster had been given in fee under the compromise arranged between Stephen and Henry of Anjou. The grant was confirmed by John in 1199,[4] and both charters were pleaded in 1292 in answer to a writ of *quo warranto*.[5] The office, which was accompanied by a holding of land, descended in the Walton family until the reign of Henry IV, and was not apparently radically affected by the events next related.

In 1229 Henry III granted all his lands between Ribble and Mersey, including the three wapentakes of West Derby, Salford and Leyland, to Randle earl of Chester, in fee, for a nominal rent of a goshawk or 40*s*.[6] The earl thus became lord of these three hundreds and evidently, as will be seen, appointed his own staff of serjeants of the peace to act within his lordships, but probably subject to the over-riding jurisdiction of the king's hereditary master serjeants in each hundred, as they do not seem to have been superseded. The earl died in 1232 and his Lancashire fee was allotted to William de Ferrers, earl of Derby, in right of his wife who was one of the heirs.[7] De Ferrers was already keeper of the ward of the castles of Lancaster and

---

[1] *Fode*, archaic form of food, fodder; see below the definition of the service of serjeant's *fode* by the tenant of Kirkby Ireleth (p. 56). It seems clear that the references to serjeant's *fold* are to the same thing and that it is not connected with the foldage, which an inq. of 1322 shows that the master serjeant of West Derby took of $\frac{1}{2}d$. a night in winter and $\frac{1}{4}d$. in summer for each beast impounded for execution (Farrer, *Lancs. Inquests*, ii, 47).

[2] See below, p. 82.   [3] Appendix III, no. 30.   [4] *Ib.*
[5] *Plac. de Q.W.*, 382.   [6] *Cal. Charter Roll*, i, 101.
[7] See my "The End of the Norman Earldom of Chester" (*Eng. Hist. Rev.*, 35, 1920).

West Derby and *custos* of the county, and his position became one of enormous power which he seems to have abused. In 1241 his three wapentakes were seized into the king's hands owing to transgressions (of some unstated nature) by the earl and his bailiffs. When restored in a year or so, the king made a specific reservation of the pleas of the crown, all cattle detained against pledge and surety, and all attachments belonging to pleas of the crown. This suggests that de Ferrers had infringed upon such royal rights, as does the further stipulation that the sheriff and coroners were to have entry into the wapentakes to make inquiry of all royal pleas, and those of the peace. The earl agreed to treat his men between Ribble and Mersey as regards pleas of the forest and all other pleas as they had been treated and used in the time of King John and up to the grant of 1229 to the earl of Chester, and to claim from them only the liberties and customs in those wapentakes which had been taken by those who had held the wapentakes before that date.[1]

De Ferrers died in 1247 and a year earlier the jury of the wapentake of West Derby had reported to the justices in eyre that William de Walton was chief serjeant, holding the serjeant's oxgangs by charter and doing the service with one horseman and one man on foot.[2] It seems likely that this special report was made in consequence of a royal order to these justices that they should diligently inquire whether to the king, or to some other person, belonged the appointment of the serjeant of the peace in the county commonly called " grit serjaunt." If the right was the king's, all those who hindered John de Holm, whom the king had sent thither to enjoy the office, were to be so chastised by fines that others might learn from their example not to resist the royal commands.[3]

The new earl de Ferrers applied in 1251 for leave to hold pleas of the forest between Ribble and Mersey but seems not to have obtained this right.[4] He was more successful the same year in another respect. On 29 April an order to the sheriff of Lancashire was entered upon the Close Roll to allow the earl, as one of the heirs of earl Randle of Chester between Ribble and Mersey, to have his serjeants to keep the peace there as Earl Randle in his time was accustomed to have them. The

---

[1] *V.C.H.*, iii, p. 3, n. 8.
[2] Parker, *Lancs. Assize Rolls*, 74. The jury's findings for the other hundreds are given below.
[3] *Ib.*, 59. A jury was sworn to hold this inquiry but their return is not given on this roll.
[4] *V.C.H.*, iii, 4.

sheriff was to permit de Ferrers the same liberty and maintain him in the rights which the earl of Chester had enjoyed.[1]

Some local resistance or objection to providing puture for de Ferrers's serjeants was probably made, as on 9 July of the following year there is a further entry on the Close Roll of a royal order to the sheriff, reciting the charter allowing the earl his serjeants, but inserting that they were for the preservation of *pacem nostram*, and commanding the sheriff to force the men of the country to give these serjeants victuals and the other things which they had been accustomed to render in the time of the earl of Chester. The king did not wish that any more complaint about the matter should reach him.[2]

Matters did not however proceed smoothly, as in 1253 Alan de Windle and Thurstan de Holland, representing the men of the hundred of West Derby, complained of illegal distraints of cattle by the earl, and that, contrary to the custom of the realm, he had forced upon them a *gryth* serjeant of the hundred of his own election ; whereas it had recently been decided in the king's court *coram rege*, on a *jurata* taken by consent of the parties, that the men of the hundred had always had the liberty that they were accustomed and ought, with the consent and advice of the sheriff, to elect and appoint *gryth* serjeants who should, and ought to, keep the peace of the king, and answer for them if that peace were not well kept. The earl eventually appeared after attachment and denied the distraints. He was ordered to wage his law but seems to have died before the issue could be decided.[3] The de Ferrers interest in the hundreds of West Derby and Salford ended in 1266 when the earl of that date was dispossessed and the honour of Lancaster, includ- ing, among other units of the king's demesnes, the wapentakes of West Derby and Salford, was granted to Edmund of Lancaster and so descended.

In 1297 William de Walton was described as bailiff of fee of the crown and holder of the *magisteria serjantia* of the whole

---

[1] Appendix III, no. 31. This order was corrected on the roll by John de Lexington (custodian of the great seal) and turned into a charter. It is not on the Charter Roll.

[2] Appendix III, no. 31 (ii). This and the previous entry on the Close Roll have been used by several writers by merely quoting Baines, *Hist. of Lancs.*, who does not give his authority. Doubtless it was Dugdale, *Baronage*, i, 262, who refers to the Close Roll entries in his marginal notes.

[3] *Ib.*, no. 31 (iii) ; Curia Regis Roll 150, m. 3 ; 151, m. 4 *d.* ; 152, m. 9 (Mich. 37–38, Hil. 38 Hen. III). No record of the earlier decision has been found on rolls 146, 147A, 147B, 148 and 149 (36 Hen. III–37 Hen. III) and nothing further on rolls 153–54–55, to 39 Hen. III.

wapentake, with one horse bailiff, either himself or another, and two under-bailiffs on foot.[1] The jury of 1246 had stated that Adam Gerard had held two oxgangs of land in [West] Derby by the service (as under-serjeant) of making judgments of the pleas of the wapentake, with a man, horse and victuals when so far from home as to be unable to return daily,[2] but that the land was then held by William de Ferrers who did the service by his own serjeants. The finding in 1297 confirmed this, and added that, as regards bailiffs at will, the lord had one horse and one foot bailiff to perform *officium wapentachiæ*.

The system continued after the introduction of justices of the peace. In 1400 the Duchy of Lancaster accounts reveal the royal bailiff at work in collecting the perquisites of the county courts and sheriff's tourns, and also the bailiff of the duke, as lord of the wapentake. The latter is described as the principal officer of the sheriff (within the lordship) and his duties to be those of guarding the peace of the hundred, making attachments, collecting the rents and the perquisites of the hundred court, levying amercements and taking distraints.[3]

Puture, " bode " and " witness " were due for the king's serjeants,[4] certain townships excepted,[5] the tenants going with the bailiffs of county and wapentake to the next township to witness distraints, together with their neighbours. Puture was likewise claimed by the serjeants of the fee of Widnes [6] and for the bedells of the " baron " of Warrington, with " bode and witness " at his court.[7]

(b) The Hundred of Salford

Ellis de Pendlebury occurs as hereditary master serjeant of the wapentake in 1199.[8] In 1246 when all the serjeants of the hundreds were sworn before the justices at Lancaster, the representative of Salfordshire (probably a deputy) was Henry son of Wenne, *capitalis ballivus*.[9] The jury found that this wapentake was then in the hands of William de Ferrers who, as has been noted above, appointed his own peace officers in this and the

[1] *Lancs. Inquests*, i, 288.
[2] See also *Lancs. Inquests*, i, 26, 116, and *V.C.H.*, iii, 13, n. 15.
[3] *V.C.H.*, iii, 2. I agree with Mr. Porteus (*Hundred of Leyland*, p. 64) that this office was that of the lord's bailiff and not, as stated in *V.C.H.*, iii, 3, the royal office held by the Walton family.
[4] *Lancs. Inquests*, iii, 90. See Appendix III, no. 32.
[5] *e.g.* Bootle and Ravensmeols, *Lancs. Inquests*, ii, 80–81 ; iii, 90, etc.
[6] *Ib.*, ii, 228.   [7] Farrer, *Lancs. Fines*, i, 109, 129.
[8] Appendix III, no. 33 ; *V.C.H.*, iv, 173, 397.
[9] *Lancs. Assize Rolls*, i, 60, 73.

hundreds of West Derby and Leyland. Certain townships owed
puture, " bode " and " witness." [1] The principal feudal tenant
was the " baron " of Manchester whose serjeant of the peace
is very fully described in the early fourteenth century.[2] He
was a bailiff, the lord's serjeant, sworn to ride for him and to
superintend and view the lordship, to levy from the foreign
tenants the lord's rents and amercements, and to summon or
attach transgressors. He was called " Grithe serjeant which,
being interpreted, was *custos pacis,*" and he gave to the earl
(of Lancaster) £10 (40s. in another version) one year with another,
and ought to be maintained, with groom and horses and four
under-bailiffs, by the tenants of certain (named) townships who
should find for the master serjeant when he came, bread, ale
and victuals with other necessaries according to season, with
victuals for his groom and under bailiffs according to what was
provided in a household, and provender for his horse, upon
forewarning by any of them, or by any messenger, of their
coming. If distress or attachment should have to be made
upon any one in that lordship, each of those tenants, if he were
required for this purpose, should assist the serjeant in making
the same, and if a summons upon anyone should have to be
served by any of them or distress should not be available, each
tenant requisitioned should furnish to the serjeant his testimony
at the court baron of Manchester. This custom was called
" sarjante's folde [*fode* in another version], bode and witnesse."
If any tenant made default in any particular of such custom,
he ought to be impleaded by the serjeants in the said court
and there make amends. The duties of the sworn foresters of
Horwich are also mentioned here, with maintenance by certain
oxgangs lying adjacent to the forest, and assistance by these
tenants in watching the nesting of the hawks.

(c) THE HUNDRED OF LEYLAND

The hereditary master serjeanty in this hundred was granted
by King John, when count of Mortain, and in possession of
the honor of Lancaster (1189–99), and confirmed by him as king,
to Gerald de Clayton in 1199.[3] The jury of 1246 found Robert

---

[1] *Lancs. Inquests,* iii, 102 *sqq.*

[2] Appendix III, no. 34. Ault, *Private Jurisdiction in England,* 321,
uses this description of the *grith* serjeant, but was unaware of the wide
prevalence of the office, as he states " there is practically no other reference to him."

[3] Appendix III, no. 35 ; *V.C.H.,* vi, 1, 29. This serjeanty has been
carefully investigated by Porteus, *The Hundred of Leyland.*

de Clayton had been *serviens custodiendi* the wapentake in fee but had sold his bailiwick to William de Ferrers. The matter was for report to the justices.[1] The position of de Ferrers as " lord " in relation to this hundred has been referred to under that of West Derby.[2] Puture for the serjeants was due,[3] and " bode and witness " by a tenant of the barony of Lacy is recorded.[4] In 1350 the earl of Lancaster, as the successor in title here of the " baron " of Penwortham, released the abbey of Evesham from the obligation of puture for the sheriff's officers which lay upon the lands of the priory of Penwortham. The puture claimed by the steward of the " baron's " court during the period of its sitting had been found illegal a few years earlier.[5]

(d) THE HUNDRED OF LONSDALE

The master serjeanty was granted by King John, when count of Mortain, and in possession of the honor of Lancaster, and confirmed by him in 1199 as king, to Adam de Kellet.[6] In 1292 when this serjeanty was challenged by writ of *quo warranto*, Orm de Kellet pleaded these charters, and alleged that from the time of the Conqueror all his ancestors from heir to heir had been seised in fee of the office and the endowment of lands in Kellet which accompanied it.[7] The district was divided into two, Lonsdale South of the Sands, and Lonsdale North of the Sands. The latter was regarded sometimes as a separate hundred, and from 1127 was the jurisdictional area of the abbot of Furness.[8]

In 1246 the jury of the wapentake reported that Adam de Kellet held three carucates by serjeanty as *custos* of the wapentake and should have one mounted and one foot serjeant in the liberty of the " baron " of Furness and two of each in the body of the wapentake. At these assizes this master serjeant was amerced for not having attached, under sureties for appearance at court, the first finder of a dead body and persons who had stripped a dead man of his clothes.[9] In 1297 the staff of Adam de Kellet as bailiff of fee was stated to be six serjeants, two in Furness and Cartmel, two in Lonsdale and two *ultra Boscum*.[10] In 1228 it had been recorded that the serjeant in fee of Lonsdale must

---

[1] *Lancs. Assize Rolls*, 66.
[2] For the history of the " lords " of Leylandshire, see Porteus, *op. cit.*
[3] *e.g. Lancs. Inquests*, i, 269, 270.   [4] *Lancs. Fines*, i, 152.
[5] *V.C.H.*, ii, 105 ; Hulton, *Priory of Penwortham*, 36–39.
[6] Appendix III, no. 36.   [7] *Plac. de Q.W.*, 384.
[8] *V.C.H.*, viii, 2, 139.   [9] *Lancs. Assize Rolls*, 105, 107, 109.
[10] *Lancs. Inquests*, i, 294.

answer to the abbot of Furness for Furness.[1] Puture for the
king's serjeants was due twice a year from (among other places)
the holders of Slyne.[2] The tenant of Kirkby Irlith was one of
those upon whom fell the duty of feeding the *grith* serjeant of
the abbot.[3] The service claimed, termed " serjeant fode," was
*inveniendi et ministrandi ballivo abbatis honeste et congrue esculenta
et poculenta qualibet septimana una die . . . in hospitio ipsius
Ricardi in Kirkebyirlyth ad custagium ipsius Ricardi.*[4] The jury
found the abbot was not entitled to the service in this form.
In the course of the abbot's justification of his claims to jurisdiction in *quo warranto* proceedings, he asserted that the county
sheriff did not enter Furness except to execute the pleas of the
crown, which was done in the company of the abbot's bailiff,
the offenders being taken to be dealt with *coram rege vel justiciariis.*[5] In 1326 the abbot petitioned to have *retorna brevium*
so that no sheriff or bailiff of the king should enter his fees to
make summonses, attachments, or executions of writs save in
default of the abbot or his own bailiffs. It was reported that
to grant the privilege would cause no loss to the king as the
abbot would have to find bailiffs at his own cost to execute the
king's mandates directed to the abbot by the sheriff. The right
was granted in 1337.[6] Many later references to the serjeant of
this hundred occur.

(e) The Hundred of Amounderness

The master serjeanty was granted at an early but unknown
date to an ancestor of the Singleton family and descended
regularly, eventually to the earls of Derby.[7] When, in 1292,
the office here and in the hundred of Blackburn was challenged
by writ of *quo warranto*, Thomas de Singleton pleaded that he
held the manor of Little Singleton, to which the serjeanty was
attached, on a prescriptive title and this was accepted.[8] In
1246 the jury of the wapentake had reported that William de
Singleton held four oxgangs by serjeanty as *custos* of this wapentake and Blackburn, with one mounted serjeant and two foot-

---

[1] *V.C.H.*, viii, 3 n.   [2] *Lancs. Inquests*, ii, 155 ; iii, 133, 145.
[3] Appendix III, no. 37 ; *Furness Coucher Book*, i, 311 ; ii, 759, 763.
[4] *Ib.*
[5] *Plac. de Quo Warranto*, 370. In a confirmation by John in 1199
of a charter, granted by him while count of Mortain to William [le Fleming]
of Furness, of liberties excluding pleas of the crown and sword, the
reservation made was *ita tamen quod serviens noster debet venire in curiam
suam ut videat justiciam (Rot. Chart.,* xl).
[6] *Lancs. Inquests*, iii, 26–27.   [7] *V.C.H.*, vii, 69, etc.
[8] *Plac. de Q.W.*, 388.

men.[1] In 1324 William Banastre held Little Singleton by
homage and the service of performing by himself and his servants
the office of the bailiwick of the king's serjeanty in these two
wapentakes, *viz.* making executions of mandates of the king's
courts by writs and summonses, and by summonses of the
exchequer, on precept of the sheriff ; also making executions
of judgments of the county court of Lancaster and wapentake
court of Amounderness, summonses, attachments and distraints
by precept of the sheriff or keepers of the king's lands, and
executions of sheriff's tourns.[2] At Ribby there was a pinfold
for distraints of cattle taken by the serjeants and bailiffs of
the two wapentakes.[3] Puture of serjeants was due and the
tenants in drengage of Thornton were among those who found
meat and drink for the lord's foresters, their horses and hounds.[4]
There were keepers of the peace here from at least 1323,[5] and
the serjeanty of the peace lost its ancient importance. A barony
held here between 1190 and 1205 by Theobold Butler lapsed,
and no references to his baronial serjeants seem to occur.

(f) THE HUNDRED OF BLACKBURN

The master serjeanty of this hundred or wapentake was
held, with that of Amounderness, by the Singleton family and
the duties and staff have been described under that hundred.
The hundred was the jurisdictional unit of the barony of Lacy,
and the baron's court at Clitheroe became known as the wapentake court of Blackburnshire. The lord of Clitheroe had his
own bailiff to make distresses and attachments, and claimed
jurisdiction over all trespasses in the hundred and the right to
punish, except in pleas of the crown. The king's bailiffs did
not enter the fee unless the lord's bailiffs accompanied them.[6]
Puture for the king's officers was due as for Amounderness.
In 1328 the abbot of Kirkstall was excused future payment of
puture for the foresters of Blackburnshire from his manor of
Barnoldswick, Co. York.[7] In 1292 a claim was made against
a tenant of Henry de Lacy, earl of Lincoln, by an undertenant
for acquittance of puture of the earl's itinerant horse-serjeant,
and also of the duty of finding a " witnesseman " to attest the
distraints and attachments. It was alleged that the custom of
the country was that the earl and his bailiffs received puture

---

[1] *Lancs. Assize Rolls*, 97 ; *Lancs. Inquests*, ii, 112 (1324).
[2] *Lancs. Inquests*, ii, 160.   [3] *Ib.*, iii, 124.
[4] *Ib.*, iii, 112, 115. For complaints about excessive bailiffs and puture,
see *V.C.H.*, vii, 70.
[5] *Ib.*, vii, 70 n.   [6] *Ib.*, vi, 231.   [7] *Lancs. Inquests*, ii, 227.

only from residents in the wapentake, who alone were admissible as " witnessmen," and that no resident could acquit another. The jury confirmed this, adding that puture " of goodwill " had been so taken of resident tenants from time immemorial.[1]

Henry de Lacy, constable of Chester, gave to his free men of Blackburnshire quittance of the accustomed puture for the horse and groom of his chief forester, and granted that, though his ancestors used to have two mounted serjeants and two on foot, there should henceforth be only one mounted, with a groom to guard his horse, and one on foot, at the charge of the country.[2] In 1351 Henry, earl of Lancaster, acquitted Whalley Abbey of puture of foresters in Blackburnshire.[3] The abbey was among the assignees of the earl's bailiwick of the wapentake who had to find a horseman and two footmen to perform the office ; they were presented yearly before the earl's steward at the court of Clitheroe.[4]

(2) WESTMORLAND, CUMBERLAND, DURHAM AND NORTHUMBERLAND

That the system extended still farther north, and was of much the same kind, is shown by some references to it in Westmorland, Cumberland, Durham and Northumberland. Further research would doubtless afford other illustrative evidence.

(a) WESTMORLAND

There is a statement in 1227 [5] of the duties of the two mounted serjeants of the hereditary sheriff of Westmorland in the lands of the " baron " of Kendal, who perambulated there on matters of the king and the sheriff, and for securing and preserving the peace. They had sworn in full county court that they would not trouble or unjustly harm any men or treat them contrary to custom. They should not collect sheaves in autumn, or exact lambs, or cause extortion. Where they took hospitality, they should behave with moderation, and not molest the host of an honest house, or take money for remitting such hospitality. All men living in Westmorland outside Kendal must faithfully help the serjeants to keep the peace and to do their business. The men of Kendal should serve summonses for suits moved

---

[1] *Lancs. Court Rolls*, xii.   [2] *Whalley Coucher Book*, 1161.
[3] *Ib.*, 1147.
[4] *Ib.*, 1164. For further details of puture in Blackburnshire, see Tupling, *Economic History of Rossendale*, 13–14. A fifteenth-century serjeants' puture roll for Blackburnshire was printed by Mr. H. Ince Anderton in *Trans. Hist. Soc. Lancs. & Chesh.*, 64, p. 273.
[5] *Lancs. Court Rolls*, p. x.

there, but ought not to be drawn to remote parts of Westmorland for these or other light causes.

In 1278, on a complaint by the people in Westmorland that the sheriff " of fee " arrested baronial men without good cause and kept them in prison until heavy bail was forthcoming, the reply was that, from the time of King John, the custom had been that if the sworn serjeant found a suspected thief or other malefactor within a barony, he attached him for appearance under sureties at the county court until the *recognitio* of the four neighbouring townships was taken. If the suspect could not find such sureties the serjeant could take him to prison until the gaol was delivered. The hereditary sheriff, Roger de Clifford, disclaimed the right to have more than four serjeants (two mounted and two on foot) in the barony to do the business of the king and the sheriff, sworn, before the sheriff in the county court, faithfully to serve the king and the men of the barony.[1] Upon the Close Roll of 1280 are entered " Certain Statutes made by the King and his Council in the County of Westmorland," following upon complaints which had recently been made to Edward I, when he was in that county.[2] After a statement that the king, who had to guard and govern the peace and the people, willed and commanded that his peace should be common to all men who were of the peace, the document dealt with the Westmorland complaints. One grievance arose out of " the assemblies and congregations which the sheriff called his tourn," to which he summoned more often in the year than was necessary the four men and reeve of every town in Kendal and elsewhere without royal authority and warrant. That the tourn should not be held more often than twice a year and at the accustomed places had been laid down by the *Magna Carta* of 1217 and later years, and one article of the inquisitions of 1274–75 recorded in the Hundred Rolls [3] had been specially directed against abuses of this provision which seem to have been common. A most remarkable feature of these royal " statutes " for Westmorland was that they purported to curtail *Magna Carta* on this point, as it was commanded that in that county there should henceforth be held only one tourn and no more in the year, at which the sheriff and the coroners should do what pertained to keep-

---

[1] Appendix III, no. 38.

[2] Close Roll 54/98, 9 Ed. I, m. 11*d*. The original entry, in French, is very faded and discoloured but has been compared so far as possible with the translation in the *Calendar (1278–88)*, 109. The king was apparently in Westmorland, at Brough on 29 August, and Appleby on 30 August 1280.

[3] See Cam, *Studies in the Hundred Rolls* (Oxford Studies in Social and Legal History, vol. vi).

ing the peace as elsewhere in the realm. The tourn was to be held after Easter at Kendal, Kirkby Lonsdale and other places convenient and least grievous. The sheriff seems to have protested and urged that *Magna Carta* authorized two tourns a year, and that it was only in these that indictments, which had to be supported by the oaths of twelve men, could be taken. So in 1290, two tourns were allowed.[1]

A second Westmorland complaint was of grievances and abuses done by the serjeants by power of their office. For these the remedy laid down was that no loyal man should be aggrieved by attachment or fine as theretofore had happened. Anyone so taken or attached, or threatened therewith unless he made fine with the serjeants to avoid their malice, was to be bailable by neighbours who knew him to be good and loyal, until the sheriff and coroners had ascertained by general inquisition whether the serjeants' action was right or wrong. Justice should be done according to the statute and those guilty of malicious conduct punished.[2] But the king did not intend by this that the serjeants should lose their power to take and attach thieves and other notorious evildoers and their receivers, and those who by the testimony of approved men were bound to evil deeds. A third grievance of the inhabitants of the towns was that the sheriff or his serjeants had summoned them too frequently, and otherwise forced them, to be present at the delivery of prisons and gaols, and took grievous fines and amercements therefor at the will of the sheriff and his serjeants. Henceforth no gaol delivery by the sheriff or serjeants was to take place without the king's writ as used in the realm. Fines were no longer to be taken for delivering prisoners, as these had greatly aggrieved the loyal and encouraged thieves. When amercements were due, they were to be taxed in full county court by good and lawful men according to the statute and not at the will of the sheriff and his serjeants.[3]

---

[1] W. A. Morris, *Mediaeval Eng. Sheriff*, 203, giving references also for the early history of the tourn in Westmorland.

[2] The Statute 3 Ed. I, c. 15 (1275) had been directed against these abuses by sheriffs who attached and imprisoned persons accused of felony and let out those not bailable for gain. The statute laid down the offences for which bail was and was not permissible. Bail was to be by surety and not the giving of goods. Breaches by the sheriff and his men might involve loss of office and grievous amercement.

[3] The document concludes with an order that women-brewers in the county should not for one amercement brew and sell all the year contrary to the assize but should be punished according to the award of the county court as elsewhere in the realm.

Between 1220 and 1246 William de Lancaster (III), " baron " of Kendal, granted Lindeth and Gresthwaite to his cook, quit of multure and pannage, of puture, and of *withnesman, land serjandarum et forestariorum*.[1] The service due to the " barons " of Dufton from the tenant of the manor of Yarnwath included the obligation of " witnessman."[2] Many releases occur in the thirteenth century of lands in the " barony " of Kendal from puture of land serjeants and foresters on horse or foot, and of witnessmen.[3] The latter obligation was sometimes due for the foresters,[4] who could also act as witnessmen.[5] The names *serjant foed* and *baleffoyd* occur for the puture of royal serjeants and other bailiffs.[6] The provisions of the Statute of Winchester for the preservation of the peace were ordered to be enforced in Westmorland in 1287.[7]

(b) CUMBERLAND

Here also there were serjeants of the peace, and of the forest, in the twelfth and later centuries. The serjeanties of Baldwin de Penred and Ralf de Carleton were for carrying the King's writs in the county at the mandate of the sheriff.[8] Puture was due for serjeants, land serjeants and foresters.[9] This, with the duties of " bode and witness," was one of the liabilities of the cornage vills of Coupland.[10] A grant of about 1203, by Richard de Lucy to Adam de Moserthe, entered in the *Register* of St. Bees,[11] reserved the following obligations : " *Homines predicti Adæ . . . invenire debent testem forestariis meis secundum usum de Caupeland malefacta testificanda fore quando fuerint inventa de propinquiore villa et prosequenda donec placita in curia mea sint finita. Homines vero predicti Adæ . . . in villa manentes debent pascere unum landsergentem et virum suum et equum suum ad tornum suum cum communitate feodi mei inter Egem et Derwent et debent invenire predicto landsergenti testem usque ad proximam villam secundum usum de Caupeland.*" In 1203–04 a claim was made by de Lucy to have four *landservientes, custodes scilicet pacis patrie*, as well as the right to exact from his tenant of

[1] Appendix III, no. 39. [2] *Cal. Inq.*, iv, 281.
[3] Farrer, *Records of Kendale*, i, 208, 222, 300, 317, 356, 395 ; ii, 58.
[4] *Ib.*, ii, 299. [5] Appendix III, no. 40.
[6] Farrer, *op. cit.*, ii, 9, 348. [7] *Cal. Pat Rolls*, 1287, p. 264.
[8] *V.C.H. Cumb.*, i, 423.
[9] Nicolson and Burn, *Westmorland and Cumberland*, i, 107, 292 ; ii, 20 ; *Cal. Inq.*, iii, 607, and p. 345.
[10] Jolliffe, " Northumbrian Institutions," *Eng. Hist. Rev.*, 41, pp. 29, 37.
[11] *Reg. of St. Bees* (Surtees Soc.), 544–45.

Briscoe the reception, entertainment and feeding of five foresters and suit for witnessing forest offences.[1]   The staff of the *custos* of the forests of Cumberland was, by an order of 1222, to be reduced from twelve mounted serjeants who lived on the people to six not so maintained.[2]   On 26 December 1231 the serjeants of this county were regulated by royal order.   Under the heading, " Of the guarding (*custodiendo*) of the county of Cumberland by four serjeants," Henry III issued a letter patent stating that he had granted to his men of Cumberland that the county in future should be guarded for ever by four serjeants only (each to have two *homines pedites*) notwithstanding that there had formerly been more.   The sheriff was specially notified of this order and commanded to have it observed and kept.[3]

The lord of Coupland agreed in 1278 with the abbot of St. Mary, York, not to exact cornage, *pastus serviencium*, " wittnes-man," or summoners to make distraints, summonses and attachments within his liberty.[4]   The lord of Millom, when granting quittance of suit at his court to the abbey of Furness for its lands at Butterilket in Coupland, freed the monks also from puture of his foresters and serjeants and the obligation of " bode and wyttenesmen." [5]

The days of the serjeants in this county must have been numbered by 1296, when two *capitanei et custodes pacis* were appointed to whom the sheriff of Cumberland was directed to be attentive, followed by later appointments of keepers of the peace in all these northern counties.[6]

(c) DURHAM

There is evidence that the peace in this palatine county was usually in the hands of four land serjeants, the hundreds being divided into bailiwicks responsible for their puture, the carrying of their messages, accompanying them to make arrests and distraints and furnishing them with witnesses in prosecutions for breaches of the peace.[7]   In this palatinate, as in Cheshire, the functions of the serjeants must have been affected by the

---

[1] *Abbrev. Plac.*, 42.

[2] *Rot. Claus.*, i, 513.   There was a later order in 1225 to inquire whether less than twelve would be sufficient, *ib.*, ii, 18.

[3] Patent Roll 42, C. 66, 16 Henry III, m. 9, and in the printed *Calendar 1225–32*, p. 456.

[4] *Reg. of St. Bees*, 374.   [5] Appendix III, no. 41.

[6] *Cal. Pat. Roll*, 4 March 1296, 25 September, 1307, etc.

[7] Jolliffe, *loc. cit.*, 37.

appointments from the fourteenth century of conservators and by the independent action of special commissioners for the preservation of the peace.[1]

(d) NORTHUMBERLAND

The evidence for the existence here of serjeants of the type under investigation is not abundant, so far as such printed references as have been noticed are concerned. From at least the tenth century, we are told, the county was divided for administrative purposes into two districts, the northern one between the rivers Coquet and Tweed, and the southern one between Coquet and Tyne.[2] There is mention of a *servien regis* in 1256, who evidently performed the duties of a *serviens pacis*, as he is found arresting a malefactor who had robbed and assaulted a hermit. The latter, by direction of the serjeant, decapitated the robber, and before the justices in eyre the custom of the county thus to treat thieves taken with the mainour was set up.[3] As in Lancashire, the *capitales ballivi* of the two divisions of the county of Northumberland were sworn with the juries of presentment,[4] and doubtless corresponded in type with the master serjeants of the peace in the Lancashire hundreds.[5] A serjeanty which had jurisdiction in the southern area strongly resembles in some of its duties those of the peace in other counties. It was held in the twelfth century by the Byker family as hereditary. The duties included making distraints for the wards of Newcastle and for the royal debts between Tyne and Coquet, carrying the king's writs, taking and guarding the pledges for the debts, making attachments and arrests for suits of the crown when the king's serjeant could not be present, and on behalf of the sheriff, serving the justices on eyre and carrying the royal writs to the barons.[6] The claim was made for this serjeanty in 1259 that the holder was *capitalis serviens* of the king for the appointment and removal of all serjeants between Tyne and Coquet, and it was alleged that Philip de Ulkotes (who had succeeded about 1210 to the Nafferton serjeanty mentioned below) had, when he was sheriff (*c.* 1215), interfered with the performance of the duties, having delivered the royal writs to the barons, taken the custody and sale of cattle dis-

---

[1] Lapsley, *Durham*, 174, 178–79. The serjeants of the peace in this palatinate are not noticed in this book.

[2] *Hist. of Northumberland*, i, 120 ; x, 40.

[3] *Northumberland Assize Rolls* (Surtees Soc.), 70.

[4] *Ib.*, 395, 397. [5] *Ante*, p. 49.

[6] *Hist. of Northumberland*, xiii, 265–66.

trained for royal debts and often acted as coroner.[1] The inter-relation of this Byker serjeanty and that of Nafferton is not clear. The latter, also with jurisdiction between Coquet and Tyne, was one of the two Northumberland serjeanties connected with the keeping of the pleas of the crown, there being another, the serjeanty of Bamburgh, for the northern area. Both were in operation as hereditary offices in the twelfth century and probably had a much earlier origin. The service due from Nafferton is variously described.[2] In 1198 it was *breviandi placita corone versus vicecomitem et faciendi summonitiones*; in 1212 *ut custodiret placita corone* and *custodia coronarie*; in 1236 *custodia coronarie regis et officium coronatorum*, and in the same year, *pro corona domini Regis custodienda infra comitatum Northumbrie*; in 1253 *ut esset coronator*. No description of the services before 1198 seems to occur except that in 1200 they were expressed to be the same as they were before 1177. The services of the serjeanty of Bamburgh are shortly described in 1198 as *breviandi et faciendi distracciones*.[3] Besides the duties implied by the descriptions of the services, the Nafferton serjeant is found, in 1165 and later, accounting to the sheriff for the chattels of fugitives and receiving an allowance for the cost of a chain for keeping prisoners in custody.[4] The apparent develop-ment of this serjeant, from an under-officer of the sheriff's organization whose duty it was to summon by writ the pleas of the crown for the sheriff, to the status of a coroner keeping the royal pleas, is of considerable importance in regard to the history of the coroner's office, and seems to bring this Northumberland officer into line with the *servientes regis* of 1181 and later years mentioned in the Pipe Rolls and considered by Mr. Bolland to have been specially appointed to supervise the pleas of the crown and to have developed into the coroners of 1194 and later.[5] Mr. Bolland's view that the functions of coroners, if not the office itself, had emerged considerably earlier than 1194 seems to find strong support in the history of these Northumberland *servientes regis*. It seems very likely that the sheriff of the late twelfth century found it necessary to depute to one of his sub-ordinates the duty of looking after the increasingly important pleas of the crown, in respect of which the sheriff's jurisdiction was passing to the justices in eyre; that this under-officer at

---

[1] Appendix III, no. 42.
[2] I take these from *Hist. of Northumberland*, xii, 257.
[3] *Book of Fees*, i, 5; *Hist. of Northumberland*, i, 120.
[4] *Hist. of Northumberland*, xii, 257–8.
[5] *Eyre of Kent*, i, liv, iv; and Holdsworth, *Hist. Eng. Law*, i, 82.

first attended to the details of summoning, arresting or securing the attendance of the necessary parties and the keeping the records against the coming of the justices ; and that in course of time and after these duties had in some cases become feudalized and hereditary, it became evident that in the interests of the crown the office of coroner must be completely separated from that of sheriff and entrusted to persons under the direct control of the crown.

(e) YORKSHIRE

Though, for various reasons, it was expected to find evidence of the existence of the system in this county, considerable research has had a negative result so far as royal officers of the special type under investigation are concerned. The printed records alone of this county are, however, so voluminous that a comprehensive examination has not been found possible and the matter must be left open. The fact that Yorkshire was not a frankpledge area [1] made it probable that the serjeants' organization operated there, as the one or the other system of maintaining the peace must surely have been in force. It will be shown below [2] that early in the thirteenth century peace officers, apparently of a paid military type, were temporarily introduced into Yorkshire as well as into many of those counties subject to the frankpledge system where the serjeants have not been found. So far as baronial serjeants are concerned, it is possible that they are referred to in a confirmation, by Randle, earl of Chester (d. 1232), to Fountains Abbey, of lands in the honour of Richmond, by which he ordered all his bailiffs and serjeants there to maintain the abbey in its rights.[3]

---

[1] Morris, *The Frankpledge System*, 51–52.

[2] p. 69.

[3] *Early Yorkshire Charters* (Yorks. Arch. Soc.), Series ii, Honour of Richmond, pt. 1, no. 86. I owe this reference to Mr. C. T. Clay, the editor.

CHAPTER IV

THE SERJEANTS IN SHROPSHIRE

THERE is abundant evidence of the organization, sometimes with Welsh terminology, in Shropshire from about the third quarter of the twelfth century onwards. Four *servientes comitatus* occur in 1209. They had found venison in a man's house and when this was reported at the forest eyre he was outlawed.[1] A royal letter patent of 1 July 1220, addressed by Henry III to the abbot of Shrewsbury, John Lestrange and all others of the county, recalled that in the time of King John serjeants to guard the parts of Shropshire had been appointed. Later, because by reason of their number the country was heavily burdened, Henry had ordered them to be reduced to twelve. But he now heard that the community had made an agreement, by fine of 200 marks with Henry de Audley (the acting sheriff), for the total abolition of the serjeants. The royal command was that this arrangement was to be set aside, and that, as previously ordained, twelve serjeants were to act until further order.[2] A similar instruction followed to Audley.[3] Another, a little later, to the same for the removal of the serjeants [4] may not have been carried out, as the royal serjeant is found taking a prisoner in 1221.[5] The Shropshire eyre roll of that year shows that the serjeant acting in the hundred of Rainhill (who may not have been one of the county twelve) took money for excusing persons from having their cattle seized for the King's use, and that he and the bedells had set up taverns and forced people to come there for their ale. At this eyre the jurors said that Hugh Pauntulf (sheriff, 1179–89) had appointed serjeants *ad voluntatem suam pro patria custodienda*, and that there were still in the county twelve or more of them who simply lived on the men of the country. The knights said that the county would be bettered to the king's profit if these serjeants were removed. It was alleged that Pauntulf had in the first instance appointed them to guard his own land but afterwards

---

[1] Eyton, *Shropshire*, ix, 144.   [2] Appendix III, no. 43.
[3] *Ib.*   [4] *Ib.*   [5] Eyton, vi, 87.

set them to guard the county.[1] The matter was referred to
the council and in 1224, the Shropshire serjeants were abolished
until further order.[2] This explains the provision in a royal
charter to Shrewsbury Abbey of 1227 that if at any time serjeants
called *grithserjanz donerant* should be appointed to keep the
peace within the county, the abbey and its men were to be quit
of all payment (*donerettum*) to them.[3] They may have been
re-appointed, as in 1274 arrests were being made in Wenlock
by William Don and his associates, keepers of the peace under
the sheriff,[4] who however may have been the *custodes pacis* of
1264.[5]

A Shropshire case of 1293 in the Common Bench affords
some historical information of considerable importance and
interest. Walter de Beauchamp, when sued by Walter de
Hopton for illegal distraint of cattle at Hinstock, pleaded
(without it being denied) to the following effect. Hinstock
was in the manor of Wem which he then held during the minority
of the heir. The latter's ancestors in the manor had used the
custom, that, for the preservation of the peace in those parts,
they might appoint serjeants, called " grissergans " or " grith-
serjauns," in greater or less number as seemed best. These
serjeants were maintainable by the *villani* of the manor and
its members, and the men of Hinstock used to do so. The
contribution was anciently granted for the support of the serjeants and the preservation of the King's peace and was ordained
for the common advantage of the country. It was called a
servicium.[6]

The baronial and manorial serjeants frequently occur in
Shropshire. A custom called *potura satellitum* was due from
certain tenants in the manor of Ellesmere in time of peace, but
it was not levied in war time, being then involved in the general
obligation to victual the castle guards.[7] In 1272 the tenants
of the Welshry in the Fitzalan barony of Oswestry were jointly
subject to an assessment equivalent to forty marks a year to
supply the *potura servientium custodientium pacem* ; and the
custos of Oswestry included £15 5s. 6d. in his accounts of 1276
for *kylch* assessed on the manor.[8] The baron of Oswestry

---

[1] Appendix III, no. 44 ; *Select Pleas of the Crown* (*1220–25*), Selden
Soc., p. 110. By a curious slip on the part of the editor, Prof. Maitland,
the proceedings on the Close Roll of 1220, mentioned above, are ascribed
in footnote 7, p. 110, to the men of *Staffordshire*.
[2] Appendix III, no. 43.   [3] *Ib.*, no. 45.   [4] Eyton, iii, 301.
[5] *Select Charters*, 9th ed., 399.   [6] Appendix III, no. 46.
[7] Eyton, x, 245.   [8] *Ib.*, x, 331.

released the abbey of Haughmond from the *kylch* which the canons had been accustomed to render to his satellites, and a vendor of land to the abbey undertook to do suit at the abbot's court at Aston *et acquietare le keys* [*cais*] *Albi Monasterii*.[1]

In 1317 the earl of Arundel, as lord of Clun, received complaints of the excessive number of his bailiffs in the district of Tempsitt. He agreed by charter to reduce them to one *præpositus* with his *serviens*, one steward with two under-bailiffs, and one *serviens* for a part of Kerry, also to take security from all future officers to cover their trespasses; but he reserved power to appoint additional officers in the district of Tempsitt if the plan did not work well.[2] *Kylch* of 70s. a year was due to the " baron " of Wem,[3] who also held a *passagium cum potura satellitum* of 40s., this doubtless being for maintenance of the serjeants of the peace of the lords of Wem while they were customarily engaged guarding the pass of Shakelford against the entry of robbers for fifteen days before and after the feasts of St. Michael and St. John the Baptist, when the men of other counties coming in paid a *passagium* of 2d. for every cart.[4]

[1] Eyton, xi, 14, 16.   [2] *Ib.*, x, 234.   [3] *Ib.*, ix, 174.
[4] *Ib.*, ix, 134, 171 *n.*

CHAPTER V

THE MILITARY SERJEANTS OF THE PEACE

DURING the last quarter of the twelfth century a type of serjeant of the peace, of less historical interest, and to be distinguished from those discussed above, was evolved from the military garrisons of castles and districts calling for special and temporary protection in this dangerous period for the Crown. The primary function of these guards, which had their older roots in tenurial obligation but had come to be provided by mercenaries, was military action against the enemies of the Crown, whether rebels or others. But the presence, within and around a stronghold, of groups of *milites* and *servientes*, mounted or on foot, must have operated as a deterrent to the criminal and wrongdoer, and their employment as local military police was a natural development of their duty. From about 1189 onwards there are indications that the serjeants of the garrisons, so largely augmented during the rebellion of John, were being increasingly used as local peace officers of a temporary nature. It is by this characteristic of temporary and localized action, as well as by the fact that they were maintained by wages charged upon the Exchequer as opposed to the puture system whether commuted or otherwise, that this type of peace officer is to be contrasted with the regular and permanent bodies of serjeants of the peace acting in certain counties, as described above. A sudden increase of serjeants, both for garrison purposes and the preservation of order, seems to date from the time of Longchamp as chancellor while Richard I was abroad. The evidence is supplied by the Pipe Rolls. Thus we read in the roll of 1189–90 of serjeants in Oxfordshire *retenti pro utlagis* and *retenti per preceptum cancellarii ad utlagos capiendos*, and the latter description is also given to serjeants retained in Staffordshire *per diversa loca*.[1] From 1190 to 1201, the ten serjeants who from 1187–88 formed the garrison of the New Castle-under-Lyme in Staffordshire, are described as *ad custodiam*

---

[1] *Pipe Roll Soc.*, vol. I (N.S.), 10, 14, 15.

patrie pro malefactoribus [1] ; in 1190, by order of the chancellor, another body of serjeants was retained in the same county *pro pace servanda* [2] ; in 1192–93 serjeants were similarly retained in Yorkshire *ad custodiendum comitatum*,[3] and knights and serjeants in Warwickshire and Leicestershire *ad tenendam pacem*.[4] In 1193–94 there are references to serjeants paid *ad custodiam maneriorum* in Essex and *ad custodienda maneria* of the Bishop of Salisbury in Berkshire.[5] The roll of 1194–95 mentions two knights *positi ad custodiendum pacem* in the city of Lincoln, apparently then in a state of rebellion.[6]

At this point of history comes in the proclamation for the preservation of the peace issued in 1195 by Archbishop Walter as chief justice of England.[7] Under this knights were to be appointed to swear all men over fifteen years of age to the duty of assisting sheriffs to keep the peace, and the importance of the hue and cry was emphasized. It seems doubtful, having regard to the date and circumstances, whether this proclamation had any real influence or effect. This is not reflected in the Pipe Rolls and remains to be elucidated.

On the accession of John, the castle garrisons were again at once largely augmented. The serjeants maintained at York, Lancaster, West Derby and elsewhere are described in the roll of 1198–99 as *ad custodiam patrie post mortem Regis Ricardi*, while at Cambridge the constable was paid to provide armed men *ad pacem manutendam*.[8] The number of places all over England at which special precautions to keep the peace were taken at this critical moment was very large, but the rolls of the following years, 1199–1200, and 1200–01 (which are the last rolls as yet in print), show that a much-reduced demonstration of force was then being found necessary as the likelihood of resistance to the new king became less probable. Unpublished rolls of a later date may well add to the history of this type of serjeant of the peace.

The retention, on military rates of pay, of these temporary peace officers must have been expensive and the system far from satisfactory ; and, with the gradual elimination of the rebellious and their following of criminals, the preservation of the peace was probably for some years left to traditional methods. Still, the advantages of a temporary augmentation of the forces

---

[1] *Pipe Roll Soc.*, vol. I (N.S.), 38, p. 47 ; *ib.*, 2 (N.S.), 149, 252 ; and other vols. to 10 (N.S.), 162 ; and the roll of 3 John, pub. 1833, p. 46.
[2] *P.R.S.*, 2 (N.S.), 149.   [3] *Ib.*, 3 (N.S.), 57.
[4] *Ib.*, 100.   [5] *Ib.*, 5 (N.S.), 11, 256.   [6] *Ib.*, 6 (N.S.), 159.
[7] *Select Charters*, 9th ed., 257.   [8] *P.R.S.*, 10 (N.S.), 38, 71, etc.

making for law and order had been seen and recognized, and they were not lost sight of in future years. That some time before July 1238 serjeants assigned *ad conservationem pacis* in the parts of Yorkshire had been appointed is evident from an order to the sheriff exempting the men of the Knights Templars in that county from contributing to the *auxilium* for the maintenance of these serjeants, although it was known that the Templars were as ready as others to help in keeping the peace.[1] An important order, directed on 28 May 1241 to the sheriff of Yorkshire and to those of twenty of the midland and southern counties [2] (*though not*, it is of importance to observe, *to any of those in the north and west where the older types of serjeants of the peace were acting*), anticipated some of the provisions of the assize of watch and ward of eleven years later. But in this order the system of using serjeants and not constables was still put in force. A number of such officers, varying from four to eight, for each county, horsed and armed *ad pacem servandam*, were to be retained on pay from June to September 1241, to itinerate each county. Upon information of wrongdoers and peace-breakers all neighbouring townships were to rally armed to the hue and cry and join with the serjeants in the pursuit, and criminals and suspects were to be lodged in gaol. In order that honest folk should not be troubled by the maintenance of the serjeants and their men, these officers were to be paid 6*d.* a day. Watches by night were to be kept in all townships until 1 August for the arrest of wrongdoers, and all strangers and suspects were to be detained until morning. In 1242 there was an order to the *custos* of the bishopric of Chester, then combined with Coventry and Lichfield, to provide six serjeants *ad pacem custodiendam* in the county of Stafford (which had not been included in the order of 1241) and to pay them a penny a day from Easter to August. The wording of this order suggests that previous officers of this kind in the county had failed in their duty.[3]

It seems likely that this system of appointing temporary serjeants to keep the peace, which has been shown to have been in operation from at least 1189, was abandoned or superseded on the general reorganization of watch and ward which took place in 1252. Under this well-known assize,[4] in order to ensure

---

[1] Appendix III, no. 47.
[2] *Ib.*, no. 48. Yorks. (8 serjeants), Sussex, Kent, Northants, Bucks., Beds., Gloucester, Lincs. (6 each), Essex, Herts., Norfolk, Suffolk, Oxford, Berks., Warwick, Leicester, Worcester, Hereford, Notts., Derby (4 each).
[3] *Ib.*, no. 49.   [4] *Select Charters*, 9th ed., 363.

the preservation of peace, watches were to be kept in town and township by armed men, having power to arrest, and to pursue by hue and cry, strangers and suspects passing by night, for delivery to the sheriff. In each township a constable, and in each hundred a head-constable, was to be appointed, under whom all those sworn to arms were to be active in guarding the peace, but only those specially deputed for that purpose were actually to carry arms. After the establishment of these constables for hundred and township (whose history is greatly in need of elucidation), little or no more seems to be heard of the temporary peace serjeants. The constables do not however appear to have displaced the ancient serjeants of the peace in such counties as had them, but when, in 1264, *custodes pacis* for every county were ordered and given power to arrest wrong-doers, breakers of the peace and unauthorized bearers of arms,[1] the end of the whole system of serjeants of the peace, and the rise of the justices came in sight.

The military serjeant of the peace is not intended to be included in the observations made in the following chapters which refer to those only of the more normal type, with which the earlier chapters have been concerned.

[1] *Select Charters*, 9th ed., 399.

CHAPTER VI

FEATURES OF THE SYSTEM

A SURVEY of the details which have been set out in the fore-going chapters shows that the general features of the system were much the same in all areas, a body of officers, both royal and baronial, specially entrusted with the preservation of peace, the repression of crime, and the execution of the orders of the courts of justice. Those duties included the making of arrests and distraints, the placing of persons under attachment by sureties to appear for trial, the service of summonses, the carrying of official messages, and the collection of some of the profits of jurisdiction. The system in Cheshire seems to have been the most elaborately organized and developed. Here, and in Lancashire, the master serjeant's office was made hereditary; elsewhere the royal officers seem to have been sworn in before the sheriff, possibly annually. The staff varied in numbers. In Cheshire there had been as many as twenty county serjeants, some mounted, and with numerous underlings, but here, as in Shropshire, reductions were made early in the thirteenth century. In other areas the staffs were not so large.

The maintenance of the officers was by the puture system (discussed below), with local variations in its incidence, and by a share in the profits of jurisdiction as perquisites, with small rewards for the production of the heads of decapitated robbers. In Cheshire, robes by way of uniform were provided by an annual grant from the local exchequer. Over and above the county or hundredal serjeants, there were bodies of similar baronial officers and forest serjeants, with much the same duties, powers and rights within their spheres of jurisdiction.

The main feature which has been demonstrated is the existence of a widespread system, in certain parts of England and in Wales, for keeping the peace by means of this organization of serjeants. Some aspects of this system, as contrasted with that of frankpledge operating elsewhere, are set out in the last chapter.

A close examination of the detailed evidence reveals a number of matters which seem of historical importance and interest. From the point of view of legal history, the chief interest, apart from the system generally, seems to lie in the powers possessed by the serjeants of arresting on suspicion and in the part which they played in the presentment of crime. Among subsidiary matters which call for some examination are the puture system and the nature of the service of " bode and witness," which the serjeants seem to have enforced.

(a) ARREST

It seems unnecessary to do more than mention the powers of the serjeants of arresting, or attaching under sureties to appear at court, persons against whom crime had been formally presented by a jury. As the officers of the sheriff or " baron " this was their duty. It is rather their *ex-officio* powers of independent action that are of interest. No doubt they shared the duty of seizing and executing the outlaw with all others of the community, but to do the same for the robber was, at any rate in Cheshire, their special function, a reward being paid there on production of the robber's head at the exchequer. As regards the arrest of the suspected, the distinction between those indicted on suspicion and those suspected before presentment had been made, must be clearly drawn. Most presentments of a jury were merely because someone was suspected of crime by someone else. In arresting such indicted persons, the serjeants were merely performing their duty as mentioned above. But the evidence goes to show that they had an *ex-officio* power to arrest, or place under attachment, on their own suspicion, or upon that of others communicated to them. This was so in Cheshire, Shropshire and elsewhere. The Lancashire assizes rolls of the thirteenth century provide abundant evidence of persons having been so arrested on suspicion. It is also particularly evident in Westmorland where, in the thirteenth century, the custom was alleged that, at least from the time of King John, the serjeants who found a suspected offender attached him, under sureties, for appearance at the county court pending the *recognitio* of the four neighbouring townships. In default of sureties the suspect was imprisoned until trial. A royal order specially preserved this power of the serjeants to take and attach evildoers and their receivers as well as others who, by the testimony of approved men, were bound to evil deeds. Early criminal law was far from tender or nice in action and the distinctions and technical refinements, limiting the power to arrest on suspicion which were introduced by the judges from the fourteenth century onwards, were not in operation. Suspicion of unpresented crime was not allowed to pass unnoticed and peace officers to whom power to act on reasonable suspicion was denied would have been almost useless. It was on the one hand their abuse of such power that was the cause of grievance and complaints, and on the other hand, it was the denial of such power in later days that created a weakness in the administration of justice.

By the Statute of Winchester (1285) an obligation was placed upon those engaged in the night watches of township and borough to arrest and detain until morning, and to pursue by hue and cry, all suspicious strangers, and those engaged in this duty, as well as the sheriff, were exonerated from its risks. But though this act remained on the statute book until the seventeenth century, it did not provide machinery for dealing with the suspected during the daytime, and this was left to official action which, in the hands of the justices of the peace and their immediate predecessors, became seriously limited, both by the omission of specific power of arrest in the commissions of the peace and by technical interpretations of the law courts. It has been shown by Miss Putnam that by 1314 the terms of the commissions given to the *custodes pacis* included specific power to arrest suspects, but that on the accession of Edward III this power was omitted. The scheme which, in 1332, led to the temporary appointment of keepers of counties, under whom the *custodes pacis* and the sheriffs were to act, included the pursuit of suspects. The commissions themselves, however, did not confer this power but only that of arresting marauders without indictment. In 1336 commissions included power to arrest within certain areas those notoriously suspected of felonies, and were extended to give full power to hear and determine offences both by suspects and others. After 1361 the normal commissions of the peace appear to omit the power of summary arrest of suspects.[1] On the other hand, the fourteenth-century commissions of the peace in Cheshire, referred to on an earlier page, clearly extended to the arrest of those suspected of crime and rebellion.

[1] Putnam, " The Transformation of the Keepers of the Peace 1327–80 " (*Trans. R.H.S.*, 4th series, vol. 12, pp. 23, 26, 28, 29, 31, 46). Further study of this subject is being undertaken, I understand, by Miss Putnam. For the judge-made restrictions upon arrest on suspicion and the special powers of the modern police, see Holdsworth, *Hist. Eng. Law*, iii, 3rd ed., 603, and Hale, *Pleas of the Crown*.

(b) PRESENTMENT

The part played by the serjeants in the presentment of
crime is of some interest in relation to the history of indictment
generally. As there seems to be little recorded evidence of
their activity before the Assize of Clarendon (1166), this must
rest upon antecedent probability alone. But there are sufficient
grounds for a reference to the subject of *ex-officio* indictment,
the right of accusation which, it is thought, belonged to the
king's officers certainly until *Magna Carta* (art. 38) purported
to deprive them of it.[1] In commenting on that section, another
writer considers " practice was loose, the king's justices
would seem to have had the right to put suspects to the ordeal
ex-officio without the intervention of the accusing jury. Sheriffs
and others, with the Crown's approval or connivance, exercised
a similar privilege. In condemning these practices *Magna Carta*
would appear to have been to some extent modifying previous
usage." [2] It is true that these observations were made on the
basis that this article of *Magna Carta* relates, not to original
accusation, but to ordeal *after* indictment by a jury. But, as
amended in 1217, it seems open to the interpretation that it
prohibited *ex-officio* indictment without the oath of a jury
unless supported by other credible witnesses. The evidence for
ex-officio action of this kind by the officers is not conclusive
but, so far as it goes, probably represents ancient custom. In
Cheshire, in the fourteenth century, the presentation of breaches
of the peace and minor offences by the tenants and residents
within the fee of the " baron " of Halton could be made by
the bailiffs of his court and were followed up by attachment
and distraint carried out by the baronial serjeants of the peace.
Capture by them of felons led to arraignment by the steward
before the " judgers " and the suitors and to the taking of an
inquisition and verdict. The forest serjeants of Macclesfield are
found conducting the jury of presentment to view the illegal
purprestures and providing the information leading to presentment for breaches of forest law. The duties of the serjeant of
the peace in the lordship of Frodsham included the making of
presentments. The abbot of Vale Royal claimed to have serjeants of the peace in his demesne manors to arrest malefactors
and cause them to be arraigned in his court. In Lancashire,
in the early thirteenth century, the hereditary serjeants of the

---

[1] Bateson, *Borough Customs*, ii, xxxi ; Pollock and Maitland, ii, 584.
[2] McKechnie, *Magna Carta*, 2nd ed., 373–74.

peace for each hundred (or their deputies) were sworn at the opening of the assizes before the juries of presentment took their oaths. This suggests that the serjeants' oaths were not merely for the due performance of their duty but because they played some part in the proceedings which involved their sworn testimony. It seems probable that they were required to swear that the reports and evidence which they made to, or provided for, the jury were true and *prima facie* well-founded, and the oath may have extended to cover *ex-officio* presentments of crime.

A presumption thus seems to arise that *ex-officio* presentment existed after the Assize of Clarendon, and calls for some consideration of the effect of the Assize and of the views which have been taken of the early history of indictment by sworn presentment of a jury. This is generally thought to have originated in the provisions of this Assize, whereby, for the preservation of order, special inquiries in every county and hundred were ordered to be made, on the oath of a jury of the hundred and one of each township, into certain classes of crime only. The offenders thus to be presented and arrested were those locally reputed to be robbers, murderers and thieves, and those who harboured them. The trial of these persons, with the forfeiture of their chattels, was reserved for the jurisdiction of the royal justices alone. This Assize did not cover the whole field of crime and tells us nothing of the contemporary manner of presenting those offences not specially named ; and it was not until ten years later that forgery and other felonies were included as subjects of jury presentment by the Assize of Northampton. (Extant assize rolls attest that the provisions of the Assize of 1166, as regards the jury of presentment, were applied everywhere, in both frankpledge and non-frankpledge areas. In the one, juries, which in some cases represented tithing vills, made presentments, in the other area representatives of the township under no communal suretyship came to do the same. The jury of presentment was not peculiar to the frankpledge system, nor specially imposed on the tithings. Indeed, there seem to be no grounds for regarding this Assize as introducing into either area any features from the other. It was intended as a general tightening up of criminal justice and was so applied everywhere.)

The Assize of 1166 recognized that there might be persons arrested otherwise than in consequence of a jury presentment and, somewhat vaguely, provided that such were to be dealt

with in customary manner. It seems likely that this provision
refers to the capture and summary treatment of outlaws and
forest offenders rather than to a wider *ex-officio* power of arrest
without previous indictment, but the matter is not entirely clear.
Apart from this point, the Assize of Clarendon did not in terms
refer to *ex-officio* presentment nor do its provisions seem necessarily to exclude this as a procedure for the future. Some
grounds for thinking it continued, side by side with indictment
by jury, in the serjeant areas have been given, and a little
evidence of the practice elsewhere has been noticed. The Pipe
Roll of 32 Henry II (1185–86) shows that a *serviens hundredi*,
in an area where the serjeants of the peace have not been found
to be acting, was expected to make presentments of crime and
could be amerced for failing to do so. At the Northampton
pleas, held before Ranulf de Glanville and other judges, William
de Stanford was mulcted in ten marks because, when he was
acting as serjeant of the hundred (court), he had failed to present
to the sheriff a plea of the Crown which had been presented to
him.[1] A similar case in Devon was noticed in 1200, a plea
of the Crown having been reported to the justices after the
serjeant of the hundred had concealed it.[2] Besides affording
evidence that *ex-officio* accusation was practised and required,
these cases lead to the inference that, if in areas like Northampton-
shire and Devonshire, where frankpledge was in force and the
oath of the capital pledge was available for the report of crime,
a serjeant of the hundred court was required to present pleas
of the Crown brought to his notice, it must have been the duty
and function of the serjeant of the peace in the areas where he
was the active guardian of order to make similar presentments
of crime.

The procedure for the report of crime before the Assize of
1166 is obscure. The current view is that to this Assize is to
be ascribed the regular institution of the jury of presentment,
and the origin of indictment—though much earlier use of the
inquisition by jury is admitted. Now it is also agreed that the
system of itinerant justices had been in force in the reign of
Henry I, if not earlier; and it follows that, in some way, crime
had been presented for trial before such justices. It seems likely
that it was the experience and information which had been

---

[1] Willemus de Stanford reddit compotum de x m. quia, cum esset
serviens hundredi, non presentavit placitum corone vicecomiti, sibi prius
presentatum. (*Pipe Roll Soc.*, 36, 8).
[2] *Curia Regis Rolls*, i, 255–56.

acquired by earlier itinerant justices that led to the reforms in procedure codified in the Assize of Clarendon and given greater precision and scope in that of Northampton. The justices had found difficulties. Criminal acts were not being reported. The county and hundred courts were not working well, from the point of view of the royal revenue. Sheriffs and their officers were slack and abusing their offices. Remedies were necessary, and were enacted, so as to ensure the full report of certain classes of crime. There seems no very strong reason to suppose that the procedure generally was entirely new. The jury inquisition was no novelty.[1] The Constitutions of Clarendon (1164) have been treated as throwing light upon the introduction and use of a jury of presentment and from them it is evident that before 1164 laymen had been called upon to answer in ecclesiastical courts upon unsworn and private suggestions of ill-fame. The Constitutions show that there were two alternatives in procedure in such courts, which Maitland thought were ancient.[2] These were (1) an open accusation by an individual or (2) a sworn presentment by a jury of neighbours. It seems reasonable to suppose that before 1166 the same two alternatives were in operation for the presentment of crime as had been employed for charging laymen in the ecclesiastical courts, and that both individual and *ex-officio* indictment was employed.

In spite of the views of legal historians, there seems great unlikelihood that before 1166 the criminal cases classed as pleas of the Crown, which date back before the conquest, were left to be dealt with by contests of " appeal " between the parties concerned, initiated by the action of the aggrieved person alone. There was money to be made by the Crown out of the punishment of crime, which was one of the reasons for reserving its trial to the representatives of the king. Is it likely that it would be left to private initiation whether or not a criminal was put on his trial? If so, the profits of jurisdiction would in many cases never have been secured. Both official action by way of presentment, and official pressure upon private action which would secure the same financial results, seem certain to have been in operation.

Early action of this kind by the serjeants of the peace, as officers acting under the sheriff, seems more than likely when it is remembered that, long before the institution of itinerant justices, the sheriff was in effect the local royal justice, with some-

[1] Haskins, *Norman Institutions*, 196.
[2] Pollock and Maitland, i, 151, etc.

times a special commission. Before him pleas of the Crown were presented, and tried in special sittings of the hundred court or in the court of a lord to whom such jurisdiction had been delegated. Though the assizes of 1166 and 1176 purported to withdraw the sheriff's jurisdiction over such pleas, he continued to exercise it during the reign of John until finally deprived of the trial of any such pleas by *Magna Carta*. There seems reasonable grounds for the view that after 1166 *ex-officio* indictment continued, though hidden behind the veil of a formal presentment of a jury, and that before 1166 and back into pre-conquest times, crime was presented by public accusation, by individuals and by peace officers and capital pledges in their respective areas.

In conclusion a minor but not uninteresting point may be noticed bearing upon the action of officials in " informing " the jury of presentment by communicating to them the *publica fama*, the local gossip and other information, which was made the basis of a presentment. In words which have acquired a slang meaning, " the jury was given the office," that is to say, a hint or suggestion as to the course which they should take. There is ground for thinking that the expression " to give the office " arose from the practice, which may well be ancient, when taking inquisitions *post mortem*, that the *officium* or verdict of the jury upon the details of the properties of the dead man held on military tenure, a document often of a very complicated nature, was prepared beforehand by officials of the court and the legal advisers of the parties concerned, and, thus settled, was given to the jury with the necessary documentary evidence to support it, and returned by them as their formal verdict upon matters of which their own knowledge must have been very slight.[1]

(c) THE *GRITH* SERJEANT

The title *grith* serjeant, which, in various forms, occurs occasionally as that of the peace officers, has an appearance suggestive of considerable antiquity. It has been noted above as used for the royal officers in Shropshire in 1220 and 1293, and also for those of the West Derby Hundred of Lancashire in 1246–53, the " baron " of Manchester and the abbot of Furness.[2] The *grith* serjeant is mentioned in *The Lay of Have-*

---

[1] See my note in *Chesh. Inqs. p.m.* (Record Soc. Lancs. and Chesh., vol. 84), p. xi. *Officium* in this sense is not in the *Medieval Latin Word-List*.
[2] I have a note (reference mislaid) of a " fine 11 Hen. III, m. 4," *quod servientes vocati gridserjeants non intrarent feodum suum.*

lock the Dane, a piece of early English romantic verse, written, it is thought, about the end of the thirteenth century, but commemorating traditional events of the sixth century A.D. Of Earl Godric, whom Skeat identifies with Ethelfrith, king of Northumbria in 593, we are told :

> Justises did he maken newe
> Al engelond to faren thorw
> Fro douere into rokesborw,
> Schireues he sette, bedels and grevves
> Grith-sergeans, wit longe gleyves [1]
> To yemen [2] wilde wodes and pathes
> Fro wicke men that wolde don scathes [3]

Grith is a word of Scandinavian origin, having the primary meaning of general or public peace and security, though it is sometimes used for the special local and personal peaces extended to places and individuals by royal decree. No instance where *grith* is compounded with the name of any *minister* seems to occur in the Anglo-Saxon laws, but they do not mention many under-officials. The association of *grith* with *serviens* may be regarded as a colloquial survival of some earlier title for this peace officer, such as grithreeve or *grith thegn*, though those names do not seem to occur.[4]

(d) Puture

The system on which the serjeants were maintained by the compulsory exaction of board and lodging, commuted later into a money payment, has been illustrated in earlier chapters. The service is described as *putura* or *potura*, serjeants' food, *pastus servientum*, and in Welsh areas, as *victus, porthiantcais, cylchcais, pastus pencais*, and *potura satellitum*, while the term *donerettum* occurs in Shropshire. In Cheshire the obligation towards the earl's officers appears as a forinsic tenurial service, due in rotation from the holders of tenements often called *warlands*. Other names for such holdings were *terra puturæ, warlands* of the manor, three *landæ terræ* (or more) called *warlands*, and three selions of *warland* containing an acre. The suggestion has been made above that such holdings correspond with the *warlands* of Domesday Book which " defended," or exonerated, other areas from the payment of geld. They were the " outland " as contrasted with

---

[1] Spears.　　[2] To guard.
[3] " The Lay of Havelock the Dane," *E.E.T.S.*, 1868, p. 9, line 263 *sqq.*
[4] The term *grithmen* survived until at least 1342 as the name for criminals who had sought sanctuary (*Reg. of Wetherhal*, ed. Prescot, quoted *V.C.H., Cumberland*, ii, 186).

the " inland." [1] It has been seen that the freeholders or
" charterers " in Cheshire, the holders of " bookland," [2] were
not subject to puture, though they were liable to perform a
service corresponding to the Northumbrian obligation of " bode
and witness." Here therefore it is clear that the maintenance
of the serjeants, like other special burdens and duties of a similar
nature, was cast upon lands under the control of the earl, which
could, by the terms of their tenure, be forced to assume such
duties. The *Magna Carta* of Cheshire relieved the demesne
manors of the " barons " from this obligation towards the earl's
serjeants, probably because such areas were themselves saddled
with the maintenance of the baronial officers. In the northern
districts the incidence of puture is not so clear. It was due
from certain townships only in some places, from residents
within a hundred in others, and from tenants in drengage and
the successors of those in thegnage. The manorial serjeants in
Shropshire were said to have been supported, by ancient custom,
by the *villani*. Many of the estates in the serjeant areas given
to religious houses were subject to the overriding service of
puture at the date of the gift, pointing to the antiquity of this
service, and some of the demesne manors of the abbey of Chester
which were released by the earl from puture for his officers in
the early thirteenth century, had been in the hands of the
secular canons at Chester in the time of Edgar.[3] It seems to
be accepted that the custom of providing maintenance for
officials goes back to Celtic times and arrangements.[4]

(e) " Bode " and " Witnessman "

The obligation to do the service termed " bode and witnessman," with the performance and enforcement of which the
serjeants were closely associated, appears in the evidence adduced
above as a common tenurial feature in the hundreds of Lancashire and in Westmorland, Cumberland and Durham. It was
a duty, a type of suit, thrown upon certain holdings, to go
with the serjeants both to assist in, and to attest, the service
of summonses and the execution of orders for the arrest of
criminals and the seizure of their goods and chattels ; to act
as messengers ; to be present when suspects and offenders were
placed, by the process known as attachment, under sureties to

---

[1] Vinogradoff, *English Society, etc.*, 186, 195.

[2] Cf. Turner, " Bookland and Folkland," in *Essays in honour of James Tait*, 375, 377, 385.

[3] See the charter of Edgar, Tait, *Chart. of Chester Abbey*, 8.

[4] Vinogradoff, *Growth of the Manor*, 223, 282.

appear at court for trial ; and to attend at court to give testimony of such proceedings before the justice or other presiding officer. A somewhat similar duty was due for the forest officers. The word " bode " is allied with bedell or beadle, and has the meanings of messenger or herald, and the performance of such functions. " Witnessman " imports acting as witness and giving testimony of what has been seen. There is no evidence that the witnessmen themselves made presentments, though their *testimonium* was probably used as a basis for indictments. It seems quite clear that they were not the same as the doomsmen (*judicatores*) of Lancashire and Cheshire.[1] The terms " bode and witness " do not seem to occur in Cheshire records but services somewhat similar are evident there. In the fourteenth century the freeholders of the county, commonly called " charterers," were found by inquisition to be bound in rotation to serve the sheriff's summonses on behalf of the officers of the peace, the number of summonses being limited, and the area for service being confined to the hundred in which the charterer resided. The service of these summonses,[2] which probably were for juries and inquisitions as well as for attendance at court of persons attached, with their sureties, had to be attested at court by two " charterers " who were however only bound to perform this duty at the next sitting. It does not appear when this obligation was cast upon those who held by charter but, if ancient, it is noteworthy as an exception to the general rule that " bookland " was exempt from all service towards the ruler except the *trinoda necessitas*.[3]

The view has been expressed [4] that the judicial service of " bode and witnessman " is of great antiquity and that it first appears in a (slightly) pre-conquest Cumberland charter of Gospatric.[5] The reference is to the concluding words of this well-known charter, by which the grantee was given jurisdictional rights over lands in Dalston which had been previously given to another " myd bode and wytnesmann on thylk stow."

---

[1] For these, see my *Calendar of Chester County Court Rolls*; and Lapsley, in " Buzones," *Eng. Hist. Review*, 47, 1932, p. 556, etc.

[2] Cf. the form of the medieval writ directed to the sheriff, to summon persons before the justices and to bring the summoners to court to attest the service and due execution of the process.—*Rex vicecomiti salutem. Summone per bonos summonitores A quod sit coram justiciariis nostris, etc. Et habeas ibi summonitores et hoc breve.*

[3] Vinogradoff, *English Society*, etc., 195 ; cf. Turner, *loc. cit.*

[4] Jolliffe, " *Northumbrian Institutions* " (*loc. cit.*).

[5] Ed. by H. W. C. Davis in *Eng. Hist. Review*, 20, 61 ; by F. W. Ragg, *Ancestor*, vii, 244 ; and by Wilson, *Scott. Hist. Review*, i, iii.

It is possible that this means that the lands had been granted subject to, or with the right to claim, the service there of " bode and witnessman," but the more natural meaning seems to be that the words quoted refer to the ceremony of livery of seisin, and mean that the grant had been made with public proclamation (bode) and before witnesses.[1] If this view is correct the charter does not materially advance the history of the service under discussion, though the early use of the words is noteworthy. Dr. Farrer, in various Lancashire works, has referred to this service. He defines " bode " as the duty of going to court to give information of anything which had happened or been discovered belonging to the jurisdiction of the court, and " witness " as the duty to testify there to any matter on behalf of suitor or appellee.[2] " In Saxon times the Lancashire thanes were required to do ' bode and witness ' whenever the reeve summoned them. In other words it was one of the conditions of their tenure that they should carry messages or summonses or attend at the court to give evidence when required. . . . This obligation continued after the Conquest but instead of being incidental to specific estates, it was obligatory on all free tenants." [3] Elsewhere Dr. Farrer has linked up the service of " bode and witness " and other obligations with the statements in Domesday Book of the duties of the thegns in the manor of West Derby and elsewhere " between Ribble and Mersey," that if a man remained away from the hundred court or went not to a plea when ordered by the reeve, or if the reeve ordered anyone to go upon his service and he went not, fines were payable.[4]

The service of " witnessman " for the forest serjeants seems to be implied in the early thirteenth-century charter by which the freemen of Wirral in Cheshire, in return for release from maintaining the county serjeants of the peace, swore themselves to keep the peace, to maintain the forest officers, and to make " proof of guilt " of forest offences. The service is definitely referred to in an early thirteenth-century charter [5] by John de Vipont, hereditary sheriff of Westmorland, to the lords of several

---

[1] Prof. Davis's translation is " with proclamation (*bode*) and witnessmen in the same place." He dates the charter 1041–55.

[2] *Lancs. Final Concords*, i, 109 n. This inadequate definition is *not* in the document which is quoted by Farrer.

[3] *Ib.*, xii. No authority is given.

[4] " Notes on the Domesday Survey," *Lancs. and Chesh. Antiq. Soc.*, xvi, 9–10.

[5] Appendix III, no. 40.

of his manors. After releasing them from puture for his foresters and everything which by reason thereof could have been exacted on the *testimonium* of verderers and huntsmen, the right was reserved that when a forest offence occurred, the service of " witnessmen " could be demanded from the lords, and the foresters were to be appointed to perform it. The latter had to swear not to injure anyone by reason of such *testimonium*.[1] In commenting upon this charter the eighteenth-century historians of the county considered that it was a consequence of the provisions of section 38 of *Magna Carta* that no bailiff should on his own unsupported complaint put anyone to his law without credible witnesses brought for that purpose ; and that an obligation to provide such witnesses was inserted because there was otherwise no power to compel persons who resided outside the limits of the forest to appear in the forest courts either as witnesses or jurymen. It seems difficult to accept a theory which would bring the duty of " witnessman " into first operation at so late a date as *Magna Carta*. A more plausible view might have been founded upon the resemblance of this service to a provision in article 4 of the Assize of Clarendon (1166) which, in the procedure for trying robbers, thieves and murderers, laid down that the sheriff should bring such persons before the justices and, with them, were to come two law-worthy men of the hundred and township where the offenders had been apprehended, to bear the record of the county and hundred as to why the arrests had been made. There is much to be said for the view that section 38 of *Magna Carta* was only a re-affirmation of the principle that an accused person could not be put to his trial by officials unless lawful men of the vicinity, who had witnessed the arrest, were present when the " law " to be performed, whether by the ordeal, by combat or by a jury's verdict, was adjudged.[2] It might thus have been urged that the " witnessmen " whose attendance at court was enforceable by the sheriff's serjeants of the peace, represent the local testimony, formally laid down by the Assize of 1166, required to corroborate the sheriff's action.

It seems reasonable, however, on general probabilities, to give to the " witnessmen " a considerably earlier origin. Anglo-Saxon laws and customs show that evidence, of a formal charac-

[1] By another charter of the same grantor by which he released both puture of foresters and " witnessman," he undertook that forest offences should only be tried in the county court. Nicolson and Burn, *Hist. of Westmorland and Cumberland* (1779), i, 23 n.

[2] McKechnie, *Magna Carta*, 2nd ed., 373.

ter, of many acts and events was called for from, and required by, the sheriff, and also from the hundred. There was need for transaction-witnesses, witnesses to criminal deeds, to their admission before local representatives, and to the evidence afforded by a dead body, bloodshed and injuries. The due prosecution or otherwise of the hue and cry required to be testified. Stray cattle had to be reported to witnesses by the finder. Some of the special duties which the " witnessmen " are found performing must have been of importance from a very early date. There were, for example, ancient and very strict rules governing the levying of a distress and the time, place and nature of the seizure, both in judicial and extra-judicial distraint. The presence of witnesses was required here, and also to the taking of sureties for appearance at court. That the compulsory provision of local witnesses, process servers and messengers should become an incident of tenure is in accord with the history of other early types of suit, and came naturally in days when there was no official machinery to enforce the giving of evidence and the *subpœna* did not exist.

CHAPTER VII

ORIGINS

THE evidence collected may be summarized as follows. In Cheshire the existence of a hereditary county master serjeanty of the peace, with its staff, has been traced to at least 1181, and with the inference that the organization in this area must have had a considerably earlier origin. Such an office is not likely to have been made hereditary unless and until it had attained sufficient importance to be sought after, both for the position which it conferred and the rewards which it commanded. The master serjeanty of the hundred of Macclesfield was in full operation at the opening of the thirteenth century and the same inference is reasonable. In Englefield (Flintshire) a body of serjeants was imposed by the crown in 1242 and was seemingly no novelty in that region. Elsewhere in North Wales the serjeants may have followed the Statute of Wales in 1284 or that of Winchester of the following year, assuming, as was the view of Vinogradoff and others, that they did not form part of the old Welsh system.[1] In South Wales Professor Rees found them " well established " by 1282 and he regards them here as of Welsh origin, and not an English importation. Some objections to this view have been developed on an earlier page.[2]

One at least, that in West Derby, of the hereditary master serjeanties of the hundreds of Lancashire, was created before 1159 by King Stephen's son, William, earl Warenne; the one in Leyland and possibly that in Salford, between 1189 and 1199 by King John, when count of Mortain; and the serjeanty in Lonsdale was alleged to have dated back to the conquest. The dates for the hereditary serjeanties in Blackburn and Amounderness hundreds are not known, but probably they were created by one or other of the above lords when they were respectively in absolute possession of the honor of Lancaster. It seems as likely here as in Cheshire that the office had long existed before it was made hereditary.

[1] Mr. Jolliffe and Mr. Waters, as will be seen below, are advocates of the opposite view. [2] p. 45.

Serjeants were imposed in Shropshire, according to a royal order of 1220, in the time of King John, and there is a statement that they had been imposed earlier, between 1179 and 1189, by a sheriff, for the protection, it was said, of his own interests.   In 1293 there is an undisputed assertion in litigation in the royal courts that lords of manors in Shropshire had a customary right to appoint *grith* serjeants and that the obligation of providing their maintenance had " anciently " been thrown upon the *villani* by an ordinance designed for the common advantage of the country.   The Shropshire serjeants were not organized under a hereditary officer and were evidently removed and re-imposed from time to time as circumstances required.   The records collected of the system in other counties are mainly thirteenth century but its developed organization argues a considerably earlier origin.

So far as direct evidence goes there is thus none for the existence of the serjeants in pre-conquest times.   Nor does a search for traces of any pre-conquest peace officers [1] from which the organization might have developed, yield any positive results as, beyond mention of various reeves whose functions and identities are obscure, Domesday Book and pre-conquest documents disclose but few of the official classes, and none in whom a prototype of the serjeants of the peace can be recognized. It is possible that predecessors of the serjeants of the peace, who were, as has been pointed out above, sworn to ride for their lords and had military obligations, at any rate in Cheshire, in an emergency, may be concealed in some counties among the very numerous *radmen* and *radchenistres* of Domesday. There is reasonable ground for thinking that these riding officers, whose tenure came to be considered as a serjeanty, included bailiffs, reeves, stewards and similar ministers, and also officers with special duties of protecting their lords' lands against evildoers,[2] but some of the *radmen* and *radchenistres* occur in districts where the organization of serjeants of the peace has not been found, and they are everywhere far too numerous to make it necessary more than to mention them as a possible class within which some early peace officers may have been included.

---

[1] Vinogradoff, *The Growth of the Manor*, 282, does not accept the suggestion that the *fæstingmen* mentioned in Anglo-Saxon charters of the ninth century were special officers entrusted with police duties.

[2] Maitland, *Domesday Book and Beyond*, 308 ; Pollock and Maitland, *Hist. of Eng. Law*, 2nd ed., i, 286, 289 ; Vinogradoff, *Eng. Soc. in 11th Cent.*, 70–72 ; Round, *V.C.H., Worc.*, i, 250, 273, and " Burton Abbey Surveys," *Eng. Hist. Review*, 20, 280.

In a valuable study of the primitive structure of the old kingdom of Northumbria (of which Lancashire, Westmorland, Cumberland and Durham formed a part), Mr. Jolliffe has incidentally touched upon the serjeants of the peace in those regions and the maintenance and other services due to them. He sees as the unit of Saxon life there, not the manor, but large estates comprising many bondage townships contributing food, rents and jurisdictional services resembling those of the half-feudalized Welsh principalities or even some earlier Saxon lordship. These groups of townships were the basis of the Northumbrian baronies. It was, he considers, through the acquisition of delegated hundredal jurisdiction by these " barons," as a consequence of which their courts became in effect the hundred courts, that certain judicial liabilities, of great antiquity in Mr. Jolliffe's view, due from the townships, became owing to the " barons' " courts. Besides an obligation on certain tenants to provide twelve " suits," he sees the rest of the bondage tenants charged with an ancient ministerial duty of supplying puture, " bode " and " witness " to the peace officers. In this and other respects Mr. Jolliffe considers that Northumbria took much from the Britons and has many Celtic parallels and he concludes that the early English settlements there embodied much Celtic custom, and that Anglian lordship united in a distinctive Northumbrian society and civilization.[1]

In a more recent essay on the " Era of the Folk in English History "[2] the same writer, in arguing for an ancient and long-lived English pre-feudal free society, upon which the manor and feudalism were superimposed, assimilates the regions of Northumbria and Wales and, in some aspects, the south-eastern counties. He sees the communities arranged in provincial units of royal administration, the kingly local centres being maintained by the " folk," the free outlanders, with renders of corn, cattle and cash, the feasting of messengers and serjeants and similar natural dues. The assessment of the folk to these burdens is distributed by repartition upon individual groups of holdings. The king's reeve rules the provincial court to which the folk owe suit, and there are tried their crimes and torts and all their local disputes. In the eighth century this society was nearing its close and with the rise of the manor, and the interposition of a lord between the people and the king, the origins of such

---

[1] " Northumbrian Institutions," *Eng. Hist. Review*, 41. Mr. Jolliffe's whole essay should be read for a full understanding of his views.
[2] *Oxford Essays presented to H. E. Salter*, 1934.

suit and services were forgotten. Mr. Jolliffe's conclusions, so far as a pre-conquest origin for the serjeants is concerned, seem to be based upon their association in post-conquest times with the thegnages and drengages of Northumbria, the Saxon services of " bode " and " witnessman," and the maintenance of the officers by an ancient system of puture.

Mr. Jolliffe's general views for the history of Northumbrian institutions have not been challenged and may be accepted. As regards the serjeants of the peace, he does not seem to have had before him any of the evidence here given of their existence in many areas besides those formerly part of Northumbria and in Wales where he had noted them. They cannot thus be regarded as a distinctive feature of Northumbria alone, and the common civilization in which they acted was evidently one of which Cheshire and other areas outside Northumbria formed a part. There are also difficulties, as pointed out above, in the assumption of the existence of the system in the ancient Welsh regime from which a Celtic and British origin was, it would seem, partly inferred.

Assuming, however, in view of the probable antiquity of the services of " bode and witness " and of the puture system, discussed above, and on general grounds, that it is legitimate to place the serjeants of the peace, as an institution, in some such type of pre-conquest communities, grounds for their existence and employment must be sought. There seem to be several. In every primitive society there must have been theft, robbery, bloodshed, rape and murder. Even when civilization had not so far advanced as to regard such acts as offences against the community, a conception which must have grown rapidly, it was clearly the interest not only of those aggrieved but of the head of the community to prevent and avenge them. Public security was always desired. While all men must naturally do what they could to pursue and arrest the offender, the obvious and most practical method of effecting such objects must have been the appointment of officers whose special function it was to do so. When, in time, compensation, assessed by legislation and enforced by a tribunal, took the place of the blood feud as the penalty for the commission of crime, officers to secure its exaction will have been needed, especially when it included a payment to the king or lord and the defaulter became an outlaw to be pursued and slain, with confiscation of his goods and chattels. When, in addition, the local lord was himself responsible to a higher authority for the preservation of peace and order, and in default was not only amerceable but also held liable to compensate those aggrieved, further incentives for the provision of some form of police at once arose. General arguments such as these for the probability of the early existence of peace officers require little reinforcement. There are, however, some particular features in Anglo-Saxon institutions which call for notice in a search for causes contributing to the emergence of such a system.

The police tithing does not seem to provide any element for the evolution of the serjeants. It was concerned, it is true, with the pursuit and arrest of criminals, but presents no other features in common. Its communal character persisted after the Anglo-Saxon system of *borh* (to be discussed below) had become associated with it, and it is the combination of police duties with suretyship which is thought by some to have been the basis upon which frankpledge was erected.[1] In any event there seems to be no evidence that the police tithing operated in districts where frankpledge was not put in force, which are, as will be shown below, those where the serjeants have been found at work.

Stubbs suggested that it might be possible to explain the exemption from frankpledge of certain regions on the grounds that the inhabitants there were *under the pledge* of the lord of the soil at the time of the institution of the frankpledge system.[2] With this hint in mind, it will also be recalled that it has been shown above that one of the main duties found to have been carried out by the serjeants in post-conquest times was that of forcing suspected, potential and actual offenders, by means of the process known as attachment, to find sureties for their due appearance at court to answer a charge. It thus seems desirable to examine the course of early suretyship as a likely field to contribute to the development of a system of officers of the peace.

In Anglo-Saxon law and custom *borh* was the name for the personal suretyship or pledge given and exacted for the general behaviour of another and for the due discharge of penalties imposed upon him for breaches of law. The *borh* system has been described as the unique plan for enforcing law and order which was followed during Saxon rule and the chief provisions

[1] Morris, *Frankpledge System*. Prof. Davis, while agreeing that the police tithing had nothing to do with suretyship, did not think that the tithing group arose from the fusion of police tithing with the *borh* group. *Eng. Hist. Review*, 26, 367.

[2] *Const. Hist.*, 1880 ed., i, 101 n.

of Anglo-Saxon law on the subject of personal *borh* have been examined [1] for the purpose of elucidating the origin of frank-pledge. They will be used here for any light which they may throw upon the evolution of the system by which peace and order was maintained in the non-frankpledge areas. Some of the pronouncements come from laws laid down by the rulers of Kent and Wessex, but so far as *borh* is concerned there seems no ground for confining their application within strict territorial limits.

A law of Hlothære and Eadric (A.D. 685–6) was that if a man complained against another and cited him to appear in a gemot or court, the accused must always give *borh* to the other and do him such justice as was prescribed. Ine's laws (*c.* 690) included the note that, if your *geneat* steals and escapes, you should remind the one who is *borh* for him of the value of the theft, for if he has no pledge you pay. The next reference of importance is in the laws of Edward (*c.* 920). A freeman with property, when accused of theft, must be taken in *borh* by those who had commended him to his lord, that he might purge himself at the ordeal. If he knew no one who would so act, security might be taken of his property and so he might escape confinement pending judgment. Athelstan (*c.* 930) ordained respecting a lord-less man, of whom no law could be got, that the kindred should domicile him to folkright and find him a lord in the folkmote. Edmund (*c.* 943) insisted that everyone must act as surety for his men and all who were in his peace and on his land, and that all those suspected and under accusation must be placed under surety. Edgar's ordinance of the Hundred (959–75), among its many police provisions, laid down that if a man fled from justice, the compensation due to the aggrieved must be paid by the one who was surety for the absconder. Another law of Edgar repeats this. Every man must have a *borh*, who should bring him and hold him to every justice, and if anyone then did wrong and ran away let the *borh* bear the consequences. Ethelred (978–1016) laid down that every freeman must have a true *borh* who could present him to every justice if accused. Every lord must have his own household in his own *borh*. Under Canute (1016–35) everyone was to be brought into a hundred and in *borh*, and his surety was to hold

---

[1] Morris, *Frankpledge*, 16 *sqq.* The texts are to be found in Liebermann, *Gesetze der Angelsachsen*, and in the two volumes of *The Laws of the Early English Kings* (C.U.P.) by Attenborough and Robertson. Some of Liebermann's texts have been used in the ninth edition of Stubbs, *Select Charters*.

and lead him to every plea. Both Ethelred and Canute laid down that the king's reeve must place under surety those publicly suspected, so that they could be brought to do justice to those who made charges against them. The laws of the Conqueror called for every man to have a pledge to guarantee that justice was done.

Coming to later times, after the introduction of frankpledge, the personal mainpast of the lord for his men is recognized in the so-called *Leges Edwardi* (c. 1135–50) as a form of suretyship contrasting with frankpledge ; and also in the Assize of Clarendon (1166),[1] in which there are expressions which, without doing violence to their context, may fairly be considered as recognizing those two contrasting forms of suretyship. Section 10 required that in cities and boroughs lords were not to keep or receive men who were neither under the lord's mainpast for appearance at court if necessary nor in frankpledge. Though the sheriff's tourn was not enforced in the serjeant areas until the thirteenth and later centuries,[2] section 9 of the Assize, in providing that no franchise should exclude the sheriff's visitations, defined his work as being, on the one hand, the view of frankpledge, and on the other, the seeing that all men were under some pledge.[3] Bracton, moreover, shows that in his time the alternative, theoretically at any rate, for every man was still frankpledge or mainpast.

If they are approached by a mind unclouded with theories on the history of frankpledge, no one can read the regulations affecting personal *borh* without seeing that they reveal the very soil in which officials of the type under examination would grow and flourish. The whole object of the *borh* system was general public security, an idea inherent in the word *grith* in one of its meanings. The inference is strong that, in order to enforce the Anglo-Saxon peace system in its various aspects, a machinery of public security officers must have been required and have existed. It does not seem going too far to say that if it had not been for the later institution of communal as opposed to personal suretyship, the practical preservation of order and peace and the prevention and punishment of crime throughout medieval England, would probably have been effected everywhere by such direct and personal official action instead of, in

[1] Articles 9 and 10.
[2] Morris, *Frankpledge*, 48, 49, and, for Cheshire, below, p. 100.
[3] For the important destinction between frankpledge and pledge see Morris, *Frankpledge*, 2, 3, 4.

the greater part of the country, through the collective surety-ship of frankpledge.

Among the special duties which the *grith*-reeves or *grith* thegns (if titles for which there is no authority may be coined) may reasonably be supposed to have carried out in the wapen-takes, hundreds and wards, under the supervision of the pro-totypes of the sheriff as the *custos* of public security, will have been the verification that all within their jurisdiction had per-manent sureties for their behaviour, and the enforcement of the *borh* system upon all who had not. Those under the pledge of the local lords would be well known and the activities of the officers in regard to *borh* would be chiefly concerned with the stranger, the passer-by and the tramp. For these, and for the *tyhtbysig* man of bad reputation, responsible guarantors must be found, and in default the officers would detain them in custody. This would be, in effect, the early form of that process of attach-ment which the serjeants of post-conquest times are seen to have enforced, under the sheriff, over the suspected and the lawless, when, under the beneficial effect of all-pervading royal " peaces " and the stricter administration of the criminal laws, it became unnecessary to maintain otherwise than notionally the personal *borh* system for the ordinary law-abiding person.

The view has been expressed that under the influence of frankpledge, by the active enforcement of which a lord could shift much of his responsibilities for his men on to the tithing group, personal suretyship declined and that, in the frankpledge areas, its scope became limited to the members of a lord's house-hold.[1] But it is clear that, in districts where frankpledge was not enforced, the system of personal *borh* would not be similarly affected. It seems indeed that there it developed and expanded in another direction under the influence of seignorial jurisdiction. The burdens of suretyship became a source of revenue and profit in that it now became an advantage to the lord to enforce his suretyship over his men. There is abundant evidence that it became the privilege of a " baron " to claim the trial and amercement of his men in his own court on all pleas save those of the Crown and even on these if his privileges included them. This claim was founded not only on the lord's jurisdictional rights. He was his men's *borh* and so was responsible for their actions and for seeing that they were brought to justice. The circle of dependants over whom this privilege, at once a right and a duty, extended was far wider than the " baron's " house-

---

[1] Morris, *Frankpledge*, 20, 23.

hold, covering as it did all the military and other tenants free
or unfree upon his lands. This view finds support in the classi-
fication which has been made of the persons who never came
under collective *borh* [1] and hence not under frankpledge. These
were (1) those under the personal suretyship of a lord, a class
which, in frankpledge areas, is thought to have become limited
to his household circle, and, (2) the unfree, " The Anglo-Saxon
legal principle that the lord was ultimately responsible for the
dependant provided for those of unfree status." [2] Thus, when
the pledge of the lord became combined with jurisdiction there
must have been added to the duties of his peace officers the
securing, by their activities, of the profits of jurisdiction.

It has been stated that the regions to which frankpledge
was not extended (which, it may be repeated, are those where
the serjeants have been found) had never been subject to the
Anglo-Saxon laws of *borh*. If this is true, that system of
suretyship can have no bearing on the history of the serjeants
of the peace. But the view seems ill-founded and is not accepted.
It seems to be argued for on three grounds. [3] First, the absence
of frankpledge, which itself was an evolution of the *borh* system.
But it does not necessarily follow that personal suretyship (as
opposed to the collective form of *borh* which produced frankpledge) had not operated in the non-frankpledge areas. Secondly,
that there are assertions of late thirteenth-century juries which
support the view. These juries were those who were concerned
to assert to the justices that there was no murder fine, tourn,
tithing or view of frankpledge in their counties for which they
might be held responsible. To such presentations a Yorkshire
jury of 1293 added that there was then no mainpast obligation
for which anyone ought to respond, while a Westmorland jury
of the year before, in asserting the same, went so far as to
declare that none of these institutions had ever existed in the
northern regions beyond Trent. That these " casual remarks,"
admittedly added for the sake of emphasis, " made for the
purpose of carrying weight with the justices," should be used
to mean more than that there were not then, and, so far as the
jury knew, never had been, any forms of suretyship, either frankpledge or personal, does not seem reasonable. The jury could
speak from their own knowledge about frankpledge, but any
active enforcement of mainpast must have ceased many genera-
tions before. The third ground is simply an unsupported state-

---

[1] Morris, *op. cit.*, 20, 23, 26, 35.   [2] *Ib.*, 26.
[3] *Ib.*, 32, 51, 52, 58, etc.

ment that the local administrative independence enjoyed in the non-frankpledge areas had prevented the establishment of the *borh* system. While such independence may have been one of the reasons why frankpledge was not introduced, it is surely no ground for inferring the absence of *borh*. The laws of Edgar, who was not only king of the West Saxons but also of Mercia and Northumbria, applied personal *borh* everywhere, and there is nothing against the system having existed in the districts under discussion at an earlier date. The contention that it was the failure of royal authority in such areas which prevented the introduction of frankpledge could be used to support the view that the system of personal suretyship was not interfered with there for the same reason.

The fact that in the serjeant areas there was in Norman times no murder fine is worth notice. In the frankpledge districts the hundred was fined for murder if one whose English parentage could not be proved was found slain and the slayer was not produced. The strange presumption that a man was a Norman unless the contrary was shown was presumably introduced to protect the Conqueror's men. That it was found unnecessary to enforce the murder fine in certain areas, points, perhaps, not to the fewness of the Frenchmen who settled in such places, but rather to the existence and effectiveness of a police system in force there for the prevention of serious crime, to the independence from new legislation allowed to those placed in charge of such areas and to the continuance, in effect, of a pre-conquest practice that the hundreds there were not, as such, penalized for crime.

Reasonable grounds seem to have been found for placing a body of public security officers in pre-conquest communities, and the suggestion of Stubbs,[1] that the inhabitants of the regions into which frankpledge was not introduced were under the pledge of their lords, seems to have solid foundations. As in one way or another the dependants of such lords were guaranteed, and the power of such lords themselves sufficed to keep their men in order, no attempt was made to force upon them a new system.

If the presence of a special staff of peace officers in Anglo-Saxon communities is accepted, some modification will be required of the view that it is *certain* that the county and hundred courts in such times had no efficient means of compelling the attendance of parties or of enforcing their orders.[2] The process of attachment may well largely have overcome the

---

[1] *Ante*, p. 91.   [2] Cf. Pollock and Maitland, i, 43, 49.

difficulty of compelling accused and suspected persons to submit themselves to justice and pay their fines if convicted, by involving their sureties in such obligations in default of the principals concerned.

If there was need for such an organization when crime was looked upon as interfering with public security only and not as an offence against the rulers of the communities themselves unless it was committed in breaches of peace which had been specially extended by them to certain persons, localities and events, it is easy to see that the system was likely to continue when such an outlook became changed. The conception of an all-pervading royal peace, breaches of which were offences against the king, was at first of slow growth but its roots were securely planted in pre-conquest times and it advanced rapidly during the eleventh and twelfth centuries. The old system of monetary fines as the penalty for crime entirely vanishes in favour of more practical and effective sanctions. The list of criminous acts was extended, punishment became personal and unemendable and life was taken instead of money. The prevention, detection and punishment of crime, with the collection of the profits therefrom, became a more important and highly organized feature of administration.

It is at this stage that the contrasting methods adopted for the preservation of peace and order are clearly seen. The contrast is drawn in the next chapter and here it will suffice to say that in two-thirds of England a system of communal responsibility for crime is found in operation, while in the other third, the serjeants of the peace appear as the active agents for the enforcement of law and order.

The evidence shows that, while frankpledge was being elsewhere carefully enforced, the serjeants were maintained and stabilized. Not only was the office of master serjeant made hereditary in certain areas, but the system received recognition as an effective one by its imposition or re-imposition from time to time. A Shropshire jury of 1293 alleged that there had been, at a date then considered ancient, an ordinance, enacted for the common advantage of the country, providing for the establishment of bodies of serjeants for the preservation of the king's peace and for their maintenance by those dependent on the land. In the late twelfth and early thirteenth centuries the crown imposed the serjeants both in that county and in the district of Englefield, and regulated by order those in Cumberland and Westmorland. The ancient type of serjeant of the peace

H

was not superseded by the system of watch and ward imposed in other areas in 1241.[1]

The history of the serjeants is evidently bound up with that of the sheriff in these areas and as, seemingly, with the ancient sheriff they grew up, so with his successors they declined. " The whole history of English justice and police might be brought under this rubric, the decline and fall of the sheriff." [2] As the keeper of the king's peace the sheriff was responsible for the policing of the county, and in part of it the serjeants were his instruments to that end. When, by degrees, abuses of office called for the curtailment of his immense powers [3] and his criminal jurisdiction was taken away, the serjeants, like the tithing, gradually ceased to be the direct means by which the peace was preserved. Before the end of the twelfth century " we see the first germ of an institution which was destined to grow at the sheriff's expense, the knights assigned to keep the peace of the county whose successors will be justices of the peace." [4] The failure and decline of both frankpledge and of the serjeant system is attested by the fact that both of them as instruments for preserving the peace are ignored in the police statute of Winchester, which recalled the lawless conditions of the country in general and sought to throw ultimate responsibility for unprevented crime upon the county and the hundred. It has been seen that the Crown ignored the protest of 1290 of the men of Cheshire against the imposition of the new burdens when they were already saddled with the upkeep of an organization of peace officers designed, but then failing, to carry out the purposes of the statute. It is to the ineffectiveness of the sheriff and his officers as guardians of the peace that must in large part be ascribed the rise of the keepers of the peace, the special commissioners of arrest, the conservators and the justices of the peace ; and with the passing to others of that branch of the sheriff's ancient duties which covered the preservation of law and order and the punishment of crime, the serjeants sank into decline.

---

[1] *Ante* p. 71.   [2] Maitland, *Justice and Police*, 69.
[3] W. A. Morris, *Med. Eng. Sheriff, passim.*
[4] Pollock and Maitland, *op. cit.,* i, 534.

CHAPTER VIII

A CONTRAST WITH FRANKPLEDGE

It has been shown in the foregoing chapters that an organization of serjeants of the peace, more or less similar in type, was in operation in Cheshire, to its north in Lancashire, Westmorland, Cumberland, Durham and Northumberland, to its south in Shropshire and Herefordshire, and in both North and South Wales and the Marches. It is a remarkable fact that these areas (with the addition of Yorkshire where, so far, the serjeants of the peace have not been found) comprise the whole of the regions where the system of frankpledge was never in operation.[1]

As the palatine county of Chester has been considered as only "probably" among the border areas in which true frankpledge was not to be found,[2] this doubt should be dispelled. There are no grounds for it. It is not possible to see any trace of frankpledge in such Cheshire records as are at present available; though they are not of the early date when the system would have been active, signs indicative of its existence would certainly have survived in them. What is found is abundant evidence in the thirteenth, fourteenth and fifteenth centuries of that sort of jurisdiction, misnamed "view of frankpledge," which had not, and apparently never had had, any concern in the enforcement of a tithing system, but in which was exercised in baronial and manorial courts a privileged and delegated jurisdiction over certain breaches of the peace, excluding the trial of the earl's pleas of the sword. When it is remembered that Domesday book shows that in Cheshire, as in several other Mercian areas,[3] breaches of the king's special peace were paid for by a fine upon the offender, whilst in the Danized areas of England the fine was levied upon the hundreds and discharged by his neighbours; that Cheshire was practically independent of the royal authority under which the frankpledge system was enforced; that, certainly after the creation of the earldom, the

---

[1] Cf. Morris, *Frankpledge System*, Chap. II.   [2] *Ib.*, pp. 50, 53.
[3] Maitland, "The Criminal Liability of the Hundred," in *Collected Papers*, I, 234.

royal writ or order did not run there ; that the sheriff's tourn, at which the maintenance of the tithings was investigated, was unknown, so far as can be ascertained, in Cheshire until the middle of the fifteenth century and had then no links with frankpledge ; that such thirteenth-century rolls of the hundred " eyres " at present in print [1] make no reference to the system either in the presentments of the juries or the amercements at such courts ; that nothing identifiable with true frankpledge is observable in the fourteenth-century Cheshire pleas of *quo warranto* [2]; it can safely be assumed that it had never existed there.

There has been recorded in the earlier chapters all the evidence for the existence anywhere in England and Wales of the serjeants of the peace which has been found in a fairly extensive search of general printed records of all kinds as well as a few manuscript sources. Such a search cannot be exhaustive and it is not possible to assert dogmatically that serjeants of the peace (other than those of the military type) existed only in non-frankpledge districts, but it will be surprising if this is found not to be so. In addition to what has been noted, there is plenty of evidence of the existence, in several counties where frankpledge was once enforced, of various county and hundredal officers who might be confused with the serjeants of the peace but with whom, it is considered, they are not to be classed. Such are the numerous bailiffs acting under the sheriff, and in the hundreds, who doubtless performed some functions analogous to those of the special peace officers, and were occasionally mounted and maintained by the community. [3] But they are never, so far as has been found, called officers " of the peace " and appear to be normal officials of the sheriff and of the hundred or its court. They seem clearly distinguishable also from the serjeant of the peace in the hundreds of Lancashire and in the hundred of Macclesfield in Cheshire, and rank rather with the bailiffs of the hundreds of the latter county. [4] Nor were the numerous bailiffs itinerant who occur in many parts of England [5] the peace officers in disguise. This seems clear, at any

---

[1] Those of the eyres of the hundred of Macclesfield, *Chester County Court Rolls* (Cheth. Soc.).

[2] Not included in the *Placita de Quo Warranto*. See my paper in *Eng. Hist. Review*, Oct. 1934, p. 677 ; and *ante*, p. 32.

[3] *e.g.* Morris, *Medieval Eng. Sheriff*, 188, 190-1, etc. ; *Select Pleas of the Crown* (Selden Soc.), 2, 11, 15, 23, 52, 58, 62, 117, 186 ; *Rot. Hund.*, ii, 307 ; Cam, *Studies in the Hundred Rolls* (Index).

[4] *Ante*, p. 15.   [5] Cam, *Studies in the Hundred Rolls*, 149.

rate for Cheshire and Flintshire, where such officials are found at work, independently of the serjeants. Here they appear as salaried officers appointed to collect special levies of money and to perform duties ineffectively carried out by local authorities.[1]

As one of the early institutions for the preservation of the peace in force in a large part of England shortly after the conquest, frankpledge has received much attention. The astonishing and inexplicable assumption made by every writer upon the subject, medieval or later, down to the time of Palgrave (1832), that it was of universal application in England as the practical method of ensuring and enforcing the peace, is now known to be quite unfounded. But even when it became clear that in large areas the tithing system had never been enforced, historians seem to have contented themselves with seeking only for reasons for such exceptions. For example, Stubbs, as has been noticed above, thought they might perhaps be accounted for on the grounds that the inhabitants of exempt districts were under the pledge of the lord of the soil at the time when frankpledge was instituted.[2] Professor Morris, by whom the system of suretyship by tithings of neighbours has been described as one of " compulsory collective bail, fixed for individuals, not after their arrest for crime, but as a safeguard in anticipation of it,"[3] considers that the reason for its absence in some places was probably the local administrative autonomy enjoyed in such excepted regions in pre-conquest times, and that this had prevented the establishment of the Anglo-Saxon surety (borh) system upon which frankpledge was built up and made it impossible to force the tithing upon such districts.[4] Some comments on this view have been made above. The suggestion, which Professor Morris makes, that it was to compensate for the absence of frankpledge that thirteenth-century law held the township liable for responding to the hue and cry and for the capture of criminals,[5] seems inadequate, and in no way explains the original exceptions. The questions which seemingly have never been put and so never answered, are these. How, in such non-frankpledge areas, was the practical preservation and

---

[1] Ormerod, i, 185, gives a long list from 1362 to 1821 which could be added to. The appointments are calendared in the 36th and later *Reports D.K.* For a specimen see Appendix III (below), no. 24.

[2] *Const. Hist.*, ed. 1880, i, 101 n. ; and *ante*, p. 91.

[3] *Op. cit.*, 2. [4] *Ib.*, 56.

[5] *Op. cit.*, 67, giving only Lancashire evidence. For the amercement of a Cheshire township for letting a man escape see *Cal. Chester County Court Rolls*, 29.

enforcement of the peace attempted ? Was there any, and if so what, organization upon which was thrown the police duties elsewhere performed by the tithing under the superintendence of its headman and enforced by the periodical oversight of the sheriff in his tourn, or in the courts of such lords as had obtained the right to do so ? It is suggested that the answer is to be found in the hitherto unsuspected and widespread organizations of officers " of the peace," the existence of which has been demonstrated, by whose activities personal, as opposed to communal and collective, responsibility for crime and breaches of the peace was enforced.

Frankpledge has been described as doing the " work of the policeman, the bail and the prison of more civilized times." [1] Amongst the police services which each group, whether true tithing or township, was expected to perform through its headman, the capital pledge, were the following [2] : There was responsibility for the behaviour of the members of the group and for the arrest of known or suspected criminals and for their custody, with liability to amercement for escape and non-production at trial ; there was a duty to secure evidence and witnesses and of producing them to testify at court where crime must be presented ; the tithing man himself made presentments to the justices. The tithing might have to secure and take charge of felons' goods, deodands and suchlike, and could be amerced for their loss or non-production. If one turns from these well-known features of frankpledge to the organization of the serjeants of the peace, it has been shown that all of these duties were performed or enforced by or through them.

In about two-thirds of England the tithing system had been put into operation. In the other third, mainly northern and western border areas and in Wales, the sheriff relied upon a body of peace officers to do a great part of the same work. Thus two parallel but very different systems for preserving the peace existed in different parts of England and in Wales.

It is noteworthy also that the defects of the clumsy and complicated tithing organization as an effective instrument for preserving the peace seems gradually to have led to a change in the areas where it had been enforced, bringing it more in line with the other system. For it seems to have become apparent that the employment of special peace officers rather than communal grouping of men was the more effective and

---

[1] Holdsworth, ii, 3rd ed., 104.
[2] See Morris, *The Frankpledge System.*

practical method of preventing and detecting crime and so the capital pledge himself became in effect, and sometimes actually in name, a local peace officer [1] resembling the serjeants of the other system.

The relative geographical distribution of the serjeants of the peace and of frankpledge raises numerous difficult questions. It has been suggested that it is worth considering whether the boundary of the Danelaw was not originally the dividing line for the incidence of frankpledge.[2] That line however would not seem to be applicable to the serjeant areas, and the problem has not been solved. The policy adopted by the Conqueror for the outlying and border districts seems to have been to put them in charge of great feudatories more or less independent of his central administration, and to leave the details of local government in their hands. Roughly speaking, the same features [3] are noticeable in these districts, from all or nearly all of which special military and defensive duties were called for against either the Welsh or the Scots. The post-conquest serjeants are found within the great and independent franchises of Chester and Durham, and also in Shropshire and Hereford-shire and their adjacent borderlands where once earls of palatine rank and sheriffs of great power held sway. Frankpledge was not put into operation in these areas, from all of which military services against the Welsh were required. In Lancashire, which in its early form, under Roger of Poitou, had been in effect a county palatine, and where royal overlordship was not fully established until the end of the twelfth century ; in Cumberland and Westmorland, border areas, with the military duty of " endmote," which had been seized from the earldom of Northumberland, and largely vested in the early twelfth century in the earl of Chester, with independence of the crown ; in Northumberland itself where there were several great franchisal areas enjoying *jura regalia* and many lay baronies from which special border services as opposed to normal soldiering were due ; here also are found the serjeants and not the tithing ; and the same is true of the borders of Wales under the exclusive jurisdiction of their marcher lords.[4] Independence of the Crown, in greater or lesser degree,

[1] Morris, *Frankpledge System*, pp. 106, 153, etc., and Hearnshaw, *Leet Jurisdiction*, p. 91.

[2] Prof. H. W. C. Davis, in *Eng. Hist. Review*, 26, 367.

[3] For those which appear to have affected the distribution of frankpledge, see Morris, *op. cit.*, chap. II.

[4] As regards the rest of Wales we can at least say that the crown did not introduce frankpledge when it was conquered and appears to have set up the other system.

and special duties of border defence, seem then to be the governing features, and according as these were, or were not, characteristics of a given area, there is found after the conquest either the one method or the other of maintaining the peace. This accords well with the view that the operation of the Anglo-Saxon system of personal suretyship had not been interfered with in the regions not effectively reduced under a central Norman administration but left to that of great feudatories ; a view which, if the connection of the serjeants with the *borh* system is accepted, would give to both them and frankpledge a common origin, and to the former the more ancient descent.

Whether the speculations which have been made upon the pre-conquest history of the serjeants are valid or not, the demonstration of a police organization in non-frankpledge areas, forming a remarkable contrast with the system of keeping order elsewhere, calls for a modification in the generalizations that in Norman times in England " there was no professional police force," [1] and that " outside the walls of the borough there was no regular plan of watch and ward, no one whose business it was to keep an eye on men of suspicious habits or to weave the stray threads of evidence into a halter." [2]   Moreover, the powers of arrest, which were vested in the serjeants of the peace, must lead to a revision of the view that in the primitive period of legal history, the twelfth to the early fourteenth century, the law relied for the arrest of offenders upon the action of the township, the machinery of frankpledge or the responsibility of a man for those in his mainpast.[3] To the instruments and organizations upon which the law relied for this purpose in a very considerable part of the kingdom, must be added the serjeants of the peace.

[1] Pollock and Maitland, ii, 582.
[2] Maitland, in " Outlines of English History," *Coll. Papers*, ii, 460.
[3] Holdsworth, *op. cit.*, ii, 598.

THE INSTITUTION OF JUSTICES OF THE PEACE INTO CHESHIRE

(a) THE JUSTICES OF THE PEACE FOR THE CITY OF CHESTER

JUSTICES of the peace emerged in the history of the county palatine first for the city of Chester and involved nothing very new there except a change of name. We hear in Domesday Book of the pre-conquest royal " reeve " (*præpositus*) and of the earl's " minister " in the city, both of whom may have had functions as peace officers, but their powers and status are not defined. Later on, in the thirteenth century, we meet with the earl's coroners for the city, who could invoke the assistance of the county sheriff.[1] But to the end of that century the earl's justiciar continued to preside at the trial of both the county and city pleas of the sword, the city sheriffs having some minor jurisdiction only. In 1300 Edward I granted the profits of the city pleas to the citizens for a rent of £100 a year, the mayor and bailiffs being given the trial of the cases, augmented by the grant of soc, sac, infangthief and out-fangthief, and the liberty of electing their own coroners. Thus the city became independent of the justiciar and the county sheriff, its civic magnates sitting as judges ; and consequently it had its own peace officers, who evidently become, gradually, as ineffective as those of the county. The change which was made by the city charter of Henry VII, dated 1506,[2] recognized the position of the city magistrates as long having been *de facto* that of justices of the peace and gave them that official title. The charter constituted the city a county by itself and provided that the mayor, the recorder and the aldermen who had served the mayoralty, were jointly and severally to be *custodes pacis* as also *justiciarii ad pacem.* The double title was perhaps used because, though the *custos pacis* will have been familiar in Cheshire and the city authorities had long exercised the general jurisdiction of justices elsewhere, the justice *ad pacem* was not yet locally known ; but possibly there were still some minor distinctions. The charter went on to say that such persons, without any further commissions, were, within the city and liberties, to keep all statutes for the preservation of the peace, those concerning labourers or the sumptuary laws, and all other articles to be executed by justices of the peace in any other shire of the realm, with power to appoint under-sheriffs, clerks and bailiffs as freely as was then done in the city of London.

[1] *Cal. Chester County Court Rolls*, xxvii, etc.
[2] Morris, *Chester*, etc., 490.

(b) The County Justices of the Peace

As a county, Cheshire itself remained without justices of the peace as such for nearly two hundred years after they had been established elsewhere and for one hundred and fifty years after conservators of the peace had been introduced into the county. Like the first representation of the county in Parliament, the justices were due to legislation in the time of Henry VIII.

It has been pointed out above how the convenient device of *ad hoc* commissions was extensively used in Cheshire, first to supplement, and then to assume, the work of the serjeants of the peace ; and how this was followed by appointments of conservators and keepers of the peace to meet special needs and events. The *ad hoc* commission was of course not peculiar to the palatinate but had long formed part of the ordinary machinery of the common law,[1] to meet local, personal or temporary needs. But it was apparent by Tudor times that it was in those very limitations that the weaknesses of these institutions lay. That they issued for a particular purpose, even though without a time limit, and did not confer a general and continuing authority, made it necessary to repeat them over and over again. It began to be seen that a more permanent effect could be obtained by a statute than by these sporadic exercises of the prerogative [2] and it was already evident how beneficial had been the establishment elsewhere of a regular system of justices of the peace, with local knowledge and central control, both for the enforcement of law and order and the good administration of local government. Neither of these desirable ends had been successfully attained by its own methods within the county palatine and by the close of the fifteenth century it became clear that the time had come to bring it into line with the rest of the kingdom. The recognition in 1506 of the chief magistrates of the city of Chester as justices of the peace was, as we have seen, mainly a change of title, as they had long performed the duties ; but that there should be permanent commissions of justices of the peace for the county was a complete innovation. Coke is historically correct when he states that " before the statute of 27 Henry VIII, the lord chancellor of England appointed no justices of the peace, justices of quorum or gaol delivery within the county of Chester " ; but an earlier statement which he makes that the rulers of counties palatine *could* " make justices of eyre, justices of assize, of gaol delivery and of the peace " requires the *addendum* that as regards justices of the peace such powers had not been exercised by the rulers of Cheshire, if we are to look only at the use of the technical title.[3]

The Act 27 Henry VIII, c. 5 (1536),[4] best known perhaps as first introducing justices of the peace into the ancient shires of Wales, recites that manifold breaches of the peace were daily perpetrated in the counties of Chester and Flint (as also in the eight

[1] Prof. Sir Wm. Holdsworth, Introduction, pp. lvi *sqq.*, to Dowdell, *op. cit.*

[2] *Ib.*, p. lvii.

[3] Coke's statements were noticed by Prof. Hazeltine in his General Preface to Dowdell, *op. cit.*, p. xxii n.

[4] *Stats. of the Realm*, iii, 534.

counties of North and South Wales), "by reason that common justice had not been indifferently ministered there like and in such form as in other places in the realm." To the intent therefore that "one order of ministering the laws should be observed there as elsewhere," the Lord Chancellor and Lord Keeper were each given power to nominate and appoint justices of the peace, of the *quorum* and of gaol delivery, in the counties of Chester and Flint (as also in Wales) by commissions. Such justices were to have the jurisdiction and authority of justices of the peace elsewhere in the realm, and keep their sessions. An act of the same year [1] preserved the position of the justiciar of Chester and Flint, presumably because the holder of that office was already an *ex officio* justice of the peace, while it also appointed as *ex officio* justices in their own franchises, the bishop of Durham, the bishop of Ely with his steward, and the archbishop of York with his chancellor for Hexham, and their successors.

A later Act, of 1540,[2] recited that by reason of that of 1536, sessions were then kept in the county palatine of Chester as in other shires; and that the justice of Chester had yearly, time out of mind, been accustomed to keep eight county (court) days one year and another year nine, at which the gentlemen, freeholders and suitors were bound of ancient custom to appear.[3] Owing to the act of 1536 there were then in addition four quarter sessions and other petty sessions, "by meane whereof the said appearance and attendance cometh so often times and so thick together that at many times they cannot depart from the one court and attend other business scarcely one day or sometimes less but they must again ride to serve the other court, which is too painful, changeable, intolerable and importune for any man to sustaine and abide." The Act therefore provided that there should in future be only two sittings in Cheshire of the ancient county court, at Michælmas and Easter, as in the county of Lancaster. The old criminal jurisdiction of the justiciar in the county court was thus curtailed in favour of that given to the new justices of the peace, but this had an unforeseen effect in that proclamation of outlawries could now only be made twice a year, opportunity being thus given to criminals and debtors to abscond. To remedy this an act was passed the next year (1541) [4] under which the sheriff of Cheshire was authorized to hold a monthly court for such proclamations, and also for hearing civil plaints for claims under 40s., which he, as contrasted with the justiciar, had never taken before.

The performance of the duties of all these justices for the city and county soon called for special accommodation, a new common hall being erected in Chester about 1545, with room for courts kept there "by his majesty's justices of the peace every six weeks." [5]

The earliest commission of the peace for Cheshire which seems to have survived is one of 3 July 1539.[6] It may have been the

---

[1] 27 Henry VIII, c. 24.　　[2] 32 Henry VIII, c. 43.
[3] For these courts, see my *Calendar of Chester County Court Rolls.*
[4] 32 Henry VIII, c. 13.　　[5] Morris, *Chester, etc.,* p. 203.
[6] *Pat. Roll 31 Henry VIII*, pt. 2; names given in *L. and P. For. and Dom., Henry VIII*, vol. 14, pt. 1, pp. 584–85.

first as there was great delay in settling the list. On 11 January 1539/40 Bishop Rowland Lee, the President of the Council in the Marches, wrote to Thomas Cromwell, then Chancellor of the Exchequer and Lord Privy Seal, " Yesterday I received commissions for justice of the peace in Cheshire and my Lord Chancellor's letters for accomplishment of same, so I am both justice of the peace and *custos rotulorum*." [1] Evidence that the justices were at work very soon after their appointment was authorized by Parliament is provided by a Star Chamber bill, apparently about 1540, which recites that some rioters who pulled down a pound at Disley were four times lawfully indicted by twelve true men " before your justices of your peace in your said county within your quarter sessions there, holden about three weeks now past." [2]

[1] *L. and P.*, *loc. cit.*, p. 28. The names for the Cheshire commission of 1554 were printed in *Cheshire Sheaf*, iii, vol. 17, p. 86, and those for 1603 in same, ii, vol. 1, p. 146.

[2] *Lancs. and Chesh. Star Chamber Cases* (Rec. Soc.), 93, and 130.

APPENDIX II

THE WELSH JUSTICES OF THE PEACE

THOUGH the establishment, in 1478, with extensions of power and permanency in the sixteenth century, of the Council of Wales and the Marches, had produced a powerful instrument for keeping the peace and the administration of justice,[1] it was not through this organization that justices of the peace were introduced into Wales, though the way was prepared for their institution.[2] Something also in this direction had already been done by various statutes from 1414 onwards under which the justices of the peace in the English border counties were given jurisdiction over Welsh criminals within their areas. Processes also in the nature of extradition agreements were instituted by which offenders could be followed into Wales and the Marches and brought to justice.[3] These matters, while illustrating the ineffectiveness to which the system of serjeants of the peace as a check upon crime had been reduced, fall outside the scope of these notes. Only the bare facts relating to the institution of the Welsh justices will be given here.[4] Abundant material for a study of their history has in recent years become available.[5]

Justices of the peace were first appointed in Wales by the act of 1536[6] referred to above for Cheshire.[7] This instituted them, under similar terms as in that county, for North Wales, in the counties of Flint, Anglesey, Caernarvon and Merioneth, and for South Wales, in Cardigan, Carmarthen, Pembroke and Glamorgan. Some doubts were removed by an Act of the same year[8] which contained a provision that no person could make justices of the peace in any shire or in Wales or the Marches except the king by his letters patent under the Great Seal. When in 1543[9] Wales was divided into twelve shires, the new ones of Radnor, Brecknock, Denbigh, and Montgomery being added to the eight old, it was laid down that, besides the President of the Council in Wales, there were to be justices of the peace and *quorum*, and also a *custos rotulorum*,

---

[1] For this court, see Skeel, *The Council in the Marches of Wales.*
[2] An Act of 1534 (26 Henry VIII, c. 12) recites that " there be no justices of the peace nor of the quorum within Wales."
[3] 2 Henry V, st. 2, c. 5 (1414) ; 23 Henry VI, c. 4 (1444–45) ; 27 Henry VI, c. 4 (1448–49), and 26 Henry VIII, cc. 5, 6, 12 (1534). See also *ante*, p. 30.
[4] See Prof. Hazeltine's General Preface to Dowdell, *op. cit.*, pp. xxviii–xxxiv.
[5] In the National Library of Wales.
[6] 27 Henry VIII, c. 5.   [7] *Ante*, p. 106.
[8] 27 Henry VIII, c. 24.   [9] 34–35 Henry VIII, c. 26.

in each of the twelve, appointed by the Lord Chancellor. The Act of 1536 had authorized the keeping of " sessions " and that of 1543 provided that quarter sessions were to be held as in England. The number of eight justices then ordered for each county (every commission also including the President of the Council, the Council and the King's Attorney and Solicitor), was subsequently enlarged in 1693 to any number considered fitting and convenient according to the ways and methods commonly employed for such appointments in English counties.[1]

[1] 5–6 William & Mary, c. 4.

APPENDIX III

A SELECTION OF ILLUSTRATIVE DOCUMENTS

CHESHIRE

III

No. 1

CHESHIRE.   Select Extracts from Pipe Rolls relating to the
                Serjeants of the Peace (see p. 3).

1181–82.   Pro justicia facienda de vii raptoribus   vij s.
                    P.R.S., vol. 31, p. 148, with similar entries
                    in vols. 32, p. 152 ; 33, p. 28 ; 34, p. 1 ;
                    and 36 (1185–86), p. 151.

1237–38.   In emendationibus ad opus janitoris superioris
                castri Cestrie et duorum servientum itinerantum
                per partes illas ad pacem conservandam et alia
                negocia Regis ibidem facienda   xxx s.
                In liberacionibus Viviani de Dauenport et sociorum
                suorum itinerantum pro pace custod'.   xxxiv s.
                Et in liberacionibus Roberti de Chelemundell et
                Owynn et sociorum suorum custodientum pacem
                Regis per annum in Cestriescira.   lx s.
                    Pipe Roll, 22 Henry III.

1238–39.   In liberacioni Roberti de Celmundeleg et Owenij
                et Viviani de Dauenport et sociorum suorum
                custodientum pacem Regis per annum in
                Cestreschira.   iiij *l.* iiij *s.*
                    Pipe Roll, 23 Henry III.

1240.   Et xxxvj servientibus custodientibus pacem de
                Cestresiria.   iiij *l.* iiij *s.* per breve Regis.
                    Pipe Roll, 25 Henry III.

1242–45.   Et Viviano de Daueneport pro excambio parci et
                vivarii de Makefeud xxiv *s.* per annum per
                inquisitionem quam idem Johannes [Lestrange]
                inde fecit per breve Regis.   Et eidem Viviano
                iiii *l.* xvi *s.* de quatuor annis preteritis.   Et xx
                servientibus assignatis ad pacem custodiendam
                in partibus Cestrie qui recipiunt per annum
                iiij *l.* et iiij *s.* per totum predictum tempus xj *l.*
                et xj *s.* per breve Regis.
                    Pipe Roll, 29 Henry III.

1245–47.   Et in liberacioni Viviani de Daueneport et servien-
                tum suorum xxiiij *s.* per breve Regis in quo con-
                tinetur quod eis habere fac' liberaciones statutas
                temporibus Ranulphi et Johannis comitum Cestrie.
                Et eisdem xxiiij *s.* de anno preterito.
                Et in liberacionibus xx servientum custodientum
                pacem lx *s.* per breve Regis in quo continetur
                quod similiter habere fac' eisdem liberaciones
                statutas temporibus eorundem comitum.
                Et eisdem servientibus lx *s.* de anno preterito.
                    Pipe Roll, 31 Henry III.

1275–76.   Et servientibus pacis in comitatu Cestrie pro
                amputacione vj capitum latronum qui percipiunt
                de consuetudine pro quolibet capite latronis
                amputato xii *d.*   vj *s.*
                    Pipe Roll, 5 Edward I.

I

1276–77.   Et Uriano de Sancto Petro pro trigenta solidis
annuis quos percipere consuevit ad scaccarium
Regis Cestrie pro mantellis ad opus quorundam
servientum custodiendum pacem in partibus
Marchie et etiam pro arreragio trigenta solidorum.

iiij l. x s.

Pipe Roll, 8 Edward I.

(For later payments of fees for robbers' heads see
Chesh. Chamberlains' Accts., 1301–60 (Rec. Soc.
Lancs. and Chesh.), pp. 6, 24, 86, 93.)

No. 2

CHESHIRE.   The right of the Serjeants of the Peace to "pelf."
Temp. Edward II (see p. 6).

David de Buskill was summoned to answer to the lord the King
for that, when Richard Wistanston, the coroner of the Hundred
of Wich Malbank [Nantwich] seized into the King's hands the
goods of Robert son of William le Berch of Hatherton (who had
fled on account of his felony) and had committed the said goods
and chattels to the township of Hatherton for safe custody on
behalf of the King, the said David, with Jordan del Hough and
other his associates, under-serjeants of the peace to Richard de
Sutton, forcibly seized, carried away and removed the said goods
and chattels, namely, corn, cloth, oxen, cows and sheep, etc., to
the value of £5, in contempt of the lord the King. And David
came and denied all his contempt and said that there is a certain
custom in these parts that, when anyone commits a felony or takes
to flight and the serjeants of the peace take possession of his goods
and chattels before they are seized by the sheriff or coroner, they
are accustomed to take a fee called " pelfre " for the capture and
taking the said goods to Chester castle. And he said that he and
his associates, as serjeants of the peace to Richard de Sutton,
seized the goods of the said Robert before they were taken by any
other officer of the King, as was lawful, and that they sent to
Chester castle that part which belonged to the King, retaining as
their fee what is called " pelfre " according to the custom. And
Richard Wistanston, who appeared for the crown, said that after
the goods of any felon had been seized by the sheriff or coroner
into the hands of the King and committed into the custody of the
township, it was not lawful for anyone to seize the same or to
remove or take them away, and this he was prepared to prove
on behalf of the crown. And the said David pleaded that he was
unable to prove his case in the absence of Richard de Sutton whose
serjeant he was. Therefore let him have him at the next county
court.

Cheshire Sheaf, iii, vol. vii (1909), p. 16, from a transcript of an
unidentified county court roll of the time of Edward II.

No. 3

CHESHIRE.   Grant by earl Ranulf III to the abbey of Chester of acquittance of puture for serjeants in its lands in Wirral, with reservation of right to increase the number of serjeants in war time. 1181–1232 (see p. 8).

Ranulphus comes sextus dedit monachis Cestrie imperpetuum quietanciam tocius terre sue de Wirall' de pultura seruientum, exceptis tantum sex forestariis peditibus et sine sequela. Ita tamen quod quatuor dominica sua maneria, scilicet Sutton, Estham, Brombur' et Irreby, quieta erunt tam de predictis forestariis pascendis quam de aliis. Et si forte, guerra urgente, oporteat plures seruientes apponi, homines de terra sua in Wyrall' apponent quantum eos continget ad seruientes illos inueniendos et pascendos, exceptis dictis quatuor maneriis que inde sunt libera et quieta.

Chartulary of Chester Abbey, 235–36.

No. 4

CHESHIRE.   Acquittance to the abbey of Chester by John, earl of Chester, of puture for his serjeants at certain places and times. 1233–37 (see p. 8).

Insuper ego ipse do, concedo et presenti scripto confirmo predictis abbati et monachis quietanciam . . . de pultura seruientum in villis suis, scilicet Huntindun, Cheuelee, Idinghale [et] Wiruin tempore pacis et Presteburi et Gorestre inperpetuum.

Chartulary of Chester Abbey, 81.

No. 5

CHESHIRE.   Acquittance by the Master Serjeant of the Peace of the abbey of Whalley from puture for serjeants in Willington. 1307–12 (see p. 8).

Notum sit omnibus [etc.] quod ego Urianus filius Johannis de Sancto Petro, serviens pacis de feodo in comitatu Cestrie, districciones in tenementis abbatis de Whalleye, quondam de Stanlawe, apud Wynlaton pro putura mei et subservientium meorum feci, ac etiam ad diligentem sequelam ejusdem abbatis per cartam domini Ranulphi comitis ipsos ab omni tali servitute liberos inveni; ob quam causam et pro salute anime mee [etc.] concessi remisi et omnino pro me et heredibus meis imperpetuum quieteclamavi eidem abbati et ejusdem loci conventui et eorum successoribus, totum jus, clameum, calumpniam et actionem [etc.] versos dictos religiosos quoad puturam illam habendam vel exigendam pro me vel subservientibus meis de se vel successoribus vel eorum tenentibus in villa de Wynlaton [etc.]

Coucher Book of Whalley Abbey, 486.

No. 6

CHESHIRE.   Acquittance by the Master Forester of the Forest of la Mare of the abbey of Whalley from puture in Willington. *c.* 1301 (see p. 8).

Notum sit omnibus, [etc.] quod ego Ricardus filius Ricardi

Doun, forestarius domini Comitis Cestrie in foresta de la Mare, pro salute anime mee [etc.] concessi, remisi et omnino pro me et heredibus meis imperpetuum quieteclamavi religiosis viris abbati et conventui loci Benedicti de Whalleye, quondam de Stanlawe, totum jus, clameum, calumpniam et actionem si que vel quas habui vel aliquo modo habere potui versos dictos religiosos quoad puturam habendam vel exigendam pro me vel subforestariis meis de se vel successoribus suis aut eorum tenentibus in villa de Wynlaton [etc.]

Coucher Book of Whalley Abbey, 485.

No. 7

CHESHIRE. Claim by the Prior of Birkenhead to be free from receiving or feeding serjeants other than six foresters (see p. 8).

Prior de Birkehed summonitus fuit ad respondendum domino comiti de placito quo warranto clamat . . . quod ipse homines et tenentes sui sint quieti de omnimodis servientibus receptandis et pascendis preterquam de sex forestariis sine equo et sine omni alia secta quando cursus illos pascendi evenerit . . . Et predictus prior venit et . . . quo ad libertatem de servientibus pascendis &c. dicit quod ipse habet diversas terras et tenementa in Wirhale et quod dominus Ranulphus quondam comes Cestrie per cartam suam concessit omnibus liberis hominibus et tenentibus et in ea terras habentibus quod ipsi et eorum heredes imperpetuum quieti essent de omnibus servientibus receptandis et pascendis preter quam de sex forestariis tantum sine omni equo et sine omni alia secta. Et profert hic cartam illam que hoc idem testatur.

Chester *Quo Warranto* Roll 1 (27–31 Edward I), m. 4.

No. 8

CHESHIRE. Grant by earl Ranulf III, to Peter his clerk or other owner of the vill of Thornton-le-Moors, of freedom from feeding foresters and serjeants of the peace for ever. 1208–17 (see p. 8).

Ranulfus Comes Cestrie, constabulario, dapifero, justiciario, vicecomitibus, baronibus suis et militibus et bayllivis et omnibus hominibus suis presentibus et futuris presentem cartam inspecturis et audituris, salutem. Sciatis me dedisse et concessisse Petro clerico meo et heredibus suis, aut cui assignaverit villam de Thorntith, quietanciam de sectis comitatus et hundredi et placiti foreste et quietanciam de pannagio de dominicis porcis suis in forestis meis et quietanciam de forestariis et servientibus pascendis. Et ut hic donatio mea et concessio predictarum libertatum in perpetuum rata et inconcussa permaneat tenenda et habenda illi et heredibus suis aut cui eam assignaverit de me et de heredibus meis, eam presentis scripti testimonio et sigilli mei apposicione corroboravi. Hiis testibus, Philippo de Orreby tunc justiciario Cestrie, Hugone abbate Cestrie, R. senescallo de Monte Alto, Willelmo de Venables, Warino de Vernon, Hamone de Mascy, Radulfo filio Simonis, Ricardo de Kingesl', Joceramo de Hellesb', Gilberto bruno, Roberto de Trohford, Hugone de Hole et multis aliis. [n.d., 1208–17.]

Facsimile in *Jour. Chester Arch. Soc.*, i (N.S.), at p. 25.

APPENDIX III 117

No. 9

CHESHIRE. References to the Serjeants of the Peace in the *Magna
Carta* of Cheshire, being the grant of liberties by
earl Ranulf III to his " barons," 1215–16 (see
p. 8).

[5] Et si vicecomes meus aut aliquis serviens in curia mea
aliquem hominum suorum inculpauerit, per thwertnic se defendere poterit propter sireuestoth quod reddunt, nisi secta eum
sequatur.[1]

[6] Concedo eciam eis quietanciam de garbis et de oblacionibus
quas seruientes mei et bedelli exigere solebant.

[16] Concedo eciam eis quod in tempore pacis tantum duodecim
seruientes itinerantes habeantur in terra mea cum uno equo
qui sit magistri seruientis qui eciam prebendam non habeat
a Pascha usque ad festum sancti Michaelis, nisi per graciam ;
et ut ipsi seruientes comedant cibum qualem in domibus
hominum inuenerint, sine empcione alterius cibi ad opus
eorum ; nec in aliquibus dominicis baronum comedant ; et
in tempore werre, per consilium meum aut justiciarii mei, et
ipsorum, ponantur seruientes sufficientes ad terram meam
custodiendam, prout opus fuerit.

Chartulary of Chester Abbey, 103–06.

No. 10

CHESHIRE. Petition of the men of Cheshire for exemption from
the police provisions of the Statute of Winchester,
as they already maintained Serjeants of the Peace.
1290 (see p. 10).

Homines de Cestre(s)hyr, qui onerati sunt de servientibus pacis
sustentandis, petunt exonerari de oneribus statutorum Wynton',
ne amplius onerentur quam ceteri de regione.

Responsio. Rex non habet consilium mutandi consuetudinem
servientium nec statuta sua revocandi.

Rot. Parl., i, f. 51a (No. 67). 1290.

No. 11

CHESHIRE. Grant by earl Randle III to Vivian de Davenport of
the hereditary Master Serjeanty of the Peace of
Macclesfield, formerly held by Adam de Sutton.
1217–26 (see p. 11).

Ranulphus Comes Cestrie et Lincolnie universis presentibus et
futuris, Salutem. Sciatis me dedisse et concessisse et hac carta
mea confirmasse Viviano de Dauenport magisterialem serjanciam
de Maklesfelde, illam scilicet quam Adam de Sutton tenuit, habendam
et tenendam illi et heredibus suis in excambium terre de Wilewic
quam mihi reddidit cum omnibus pertinenciis suis. Ita scilicet
quod si idem Vivianus vel aliquis heredum suorum forisfaciat, unde
non possit vel nolit pacem et gardum curie mee [? custodire], ballivam
dictam amittat in perpetuum et terra sua tota, quam de me tenet,

[1] See my article " Thwert-ut-nay and the custom of Thwertnic in
Cheshire," *Eng. Hist. Review*, 40, 1925.

in capite incurrat. Hiis testibus, domino Hugone abbate Cestrie, Philippo de Orreby tunc justiciario, Henrico de Aldithel', Rogero de Mannelwar', Aluredo de Sulinur', Thoma de Orreby, Herberto de Orreby, Ricardo de Cagwor(th) tunc camerario, magistro Hugone et multis aliis. (n.d. 1217–26.]

Enrolled 8 Jan. 1601–02 on Cheshire Recognizance Roll (*39 Rep. Dep. Keeper*, 91). Other versions in Earwaker, *East Cheshire*, ii, 379, and Ormerod, iii, 62, who adds *jure hereditatis sue* after *incurrat*.

No. 12

CHESHIRE. Charter of Randle III, earl of Chester (confirmed by Edward I), to the freemen of Wirral, releasing them from maintaining serjeants of the peace other than six foot foresters, provided that twelve serjeants should be found and kept if required and that the men of Wirral should themselves keep the peace there and in the forest, etc. 1194–1208 [1] (see p. 12).

Rex omnibus ad quos etc. salutem. Inspeximus cartam Ranulphi quondam Comitis Cestrie in hoc verba :

Ranulphus Comes Cestrie constabulario suo et dapifero, justiciariis, vicecomitibus, baronibus et ballivis et omnibus fidelibus suis tam futuris quam presentibus salutem. Notum sit vobis omnibus me concessisse et hac carta mea confirmasse omnibus liberis hominibus manentibus in Wirhallia et in ea terras habentibus de me et meis heredibus quietanciam de servientibus pascendis eis et eorum heredibus. Ita quod ipsi et eorum heredes et homines sui et terre sue de Wirhallia imperpetuum sint quieti de servientibus pascendis nisi solummodo de sex forestariis peditibus sine omni equo et sine omni alia secta. Et forestarii illi per totam Wirhalliam pascentur exceptis maneriis abbatis Cestrie scilicet Estham et Brumburg' et Ireby et Sutton'. Et si aliquid negocium in terra mea emerserit propter quod oporteat servientes tenere, predicti homines de Wirhallia invenient duodecim servientes et eos tenebunt ad custum suum quamdiu negocium terre durabit. Ipsi eciam posse suum facient de terra mea defendenda et in pace tenenda et juraverunt quod forestam meam propter posse suo legaliter servabunt et quod nec in terra mea nec in foresta mea forisfacient nec forisfieri permittent, et si scierint aliquem in eis forisfacere ipsi corpus ejus si possunt capient et illud reddent michi vel justiciario meo et si eum capere non possint ipsi illud monstrabunt michi vel justiciario meo vel ballivo meo de patria ipsa. Hiis testibus Gaufrido Abbate Cestrie, Philippo de Orreby, Hamone de Mascy, Warino de Vernon, Willelmo de Venabl(es), Thoma et Henrico Dispenser', Petro clerico, David clerico de Malopassu, Ricardo clerico et aliis multis · apud Cestriam.

Nos autem concessionem et confirmacionem predictas ratas habentes et gratas, eas pro nobis et heredibus nostris quantum in nobis est concedimus et confirmavimus sicut carta predicta ration-

---

[1] The date limits are fixed by the abbacy of Geoffrey, abbot of Chester, **one of the** witnesses.

abiliter testatur. In cujus &c. Teste apud Carlaverok, x die
Julii 28 Edward I. [1300]. per finem factum in scaccario.
Patent Roll, C. 66, 120, m. 10 (28 Edward I).

No. 13

CHESHIRE. Release by the hereditary Master Forester of Wirral
of lands at Hooton from puture money for forest
serjeants, after the disafforestation of 1376. 23 June
1377 (see p. 13).

A touz iceux que ceste escript verrount ou orrount, William
filz William filz Johan de Stanley de Wyrhale leisne, Saluz en Dieu.
Sachez moi par ceste escript avoir relesse graunte et conferme et
pour moi et pour mes heirs quiteclame a William de Hoton et a
sez heirs a touz iours totes maneres de putures profitz rentes et
deniers pour putures et totes maneres charges qeconqes par cause
dez putures lez qeux moi ou mes auncestres en ascune manere
avoions prendre et receyvre soloions de dit William de Hoton ou
de sez auncestres du sez terres et tenementez en la ville de Hoton
oe lez appurtenauncez en Wyrhale. Issuit que [ne] moi lavantdit
William filz William filz Johan ne mes heirs ascunez putures profitz
rentes deniers pour putures ou par cause dez putures du lez terres
et tenementez avantditz ne dascune parcelle dicelles desore clamer
ou demander puissons, mes par ceste escript soions forclos a touz
iours . . . En tesmoignance de quele chose a ceste escript ay mis
moun seal. Donne a Storton le Marsdy proschein devaunt la feste
de la Nativité de seint Johan le Baptistre lan du regne le Roi Richard
secunde apres le conqueste primer. [23 June 1377.]
Journal Chester Arch. Soc., vi (N.S.), 213.

No. 14

CHESHIRE. Grant of the vill of Chelford, at a yearly rent for all
service, saving puture for the serjeants of the peace,
etc. 1245–50 (see p. 81).

Sciant etc. ego Robertus Picot dedi etc. Roberto de Worth pro
homagio et servitio suo totam villam de Cholleford . . . reddendo
inde annuatim 7s. argenti et unum par calcarium . . . pro omni
servitio etc. . . . salvo puturo servientium pacis et clausura
hayarum de foresta de Macclesfeld, etc.
Chartulary of Chester Abbey, 319.

No. 15

CHESHIRE. Grant of land to the abbey of Chester saving the
forinsic service of puture for the abbot and the serjeant of the peace. 1265–91 (see p. 81).

Willelmus de Lautona dedit Symoni abbati Cestrie unam bovatam
terre in Lauton . . . salvo forinseco servicio scilicet pultura eiusdem
abbatis et seruientis pacis.
Chartulary of Chester Abbey, 440.

No. 16

CHESHIRE. Quitclaim of lands to the abbey of Chester, subject to the forinsic service of providing puture for two foresters thrice a year. 1265–91 (see p. 81).

Willelmus filius Colberti de Vpton quiete clamavit . . . Symoni abbati Cestrie ii bovatas terre in Wodechirche . . . quas de dicto abbate antea tenuit, faciendo forinsecum seruicium scilicet pulturam duorum forestariorum ter per annum.

Chartulary of Chester Abbey, 364, and cf. p. 362.

No. 17

CHESHIRE. Military and other duties of the Serjeants of the Peace in time of war, set out in the Inquest of Service, 1288 (see p. 14).

[49] Urianus de Sancto Petro et Rotherus filius Griffini tenent totam serianciam pacis in Cestrisira exceptis Hundredis de Maclisfeld et Wyrhale, et inveniendo [xii] servientes pedites quorum unus erit [eques] et habebit prebendam super forinsecas terras in dimidio anno [hiemali] et [ibidem servientes] custodient pacem et venient ad summonicionem domini regis custibus suis propriis in Cestrisira et quamcito transient aquam de Dee vel alibi extra Cestrisiram erunt custibus domini regis.

[50] Rogerus Daueneport tenet unam seriantiam in Hundredo de Maclisfeld, Leck et D . . . et inveniet viii servientes quorum unus sit eques et faciet servicium eodem modo quo Urianus de Sancto Petro et Rotherus.

Calendar of Chester County Court Rolls, 1259–97, 111–12.

No. 18

CHESHIRE. Claim to a Master Serjeanty of the Peace of the "baron" of Halton, and other privileges, in a plea of *quo warranto* 1350–60 by Henry duke of Lancaster, as lord of Halton (see p. 19).

Item, clamat habere aliam liberam curiam annuatim . . . et in eadem curia habere cognitionem placitorum de transgressionibus . . . et si presentatum sit per ballivos dicti ducis curiæ . . . quod aliquis hominum, tenentium seu residentium infra feodum dominii sui prædicti, fregerit pacem [etc.] quod tunc ballivi dicti ducis curiæ . . . per processum debitum, scilicet per attachiamentum et districtionem, facient eosdem transgressores venire ad respondendum in curia predicta . . .

Item, clamat habere infra feodum dominii sui predicti unum magistrum servientem, ad equum juratum, cum octo subservientibus et duobus garcionibus sub eodem magistro, juratis ad custodiendam pacem per totum feodum predictum et ad serviendum dicto duci de executionibus curiarum suarum predictarum faciendis; qui quidem magister serviens cum subservientibus et garcionibus suis predictis habere debent puturam, vel rationabilem finem pro putura eadem, de omnibus tenentibus tres landas terre, vel plures, terrarum vocatarum Warland infra feodum predictum, scilicet pro dicto magistro serviente et duobus subservientibus suis et uno garcione, cum uno tenente tenentium predictorum, coenare, pernoctare, et in die proxime sequenti ante recessum suum jentare ; et pro aliis duobus subservientibus cum uno garcione, cum alio tenente tenentium predictorum similiter [etc.] ; et sic de sex septimanis in sex septimanas separatim annuatim in forma predicta cenare, pernoctare et jentare, ita quod quilibet tenens tenentium predictorum cum quo predictus magister serviens cum duobus subservientibus et uno garcione vel etiam cum quo duo de subservientibus predictis cum uno garcione [etc.] in forma predicta coenaverunt, pernoctaverunt et jentaverunt, erit quietus tam de dicto magistro serviente quam de aliis subservientibus et garcionibus predictis pascendis per sex septimanas proxime tunc sequentes ; et idem magister serviens habere debet de quolibet tenente tenentium predictorum pro equo suo unum bushel avenarum pro prebenda, capienda annuatim inter festa sancti Michaelis et inventionis Sancte Crucis.

Item, clamat quod si dicti servientes seu ballivi sui aliquem latronem pro aliquid furto ubicunque fuerit, facto cum manuopere infra feodum dominii sui predicti ceperint seu attachiaverint, et si ille latro feloniam illam coram quatuor villatis spontanea voluntate cognoverit, tunc liceat dictis servientibus seu ballivis suis dictum latronem decollare, et dictus dux tunc habebit omnia bona et catalla dicti latronis infra feodum suum predictum inventa.

Item, clamat quod si aliquis captus fuerit infra feodum dominii sui predicti per dictos servientes seu ballivos suos cum manuopere alicujus felonie, quod tunc, felonia illa cognita aut incognita, liceat dictis servientibus seu ballivis ducere dictum felonem ad prisonam dicti ducis apud Halton et ibidem illum retinere per tres curias ibidem proxime sequentes, ad quas venient omnes judicatores et sectatores curie predicte per rationabilem premonitionem, et in quacunque curia illarum liceat senescallo ejusdem curie illum felonem de dicta felonia ibidem arrainiare, et si ille felo se ponere ibidem voluerit super inquisitionem curia predicte, tunc liceat senescallo illam inquisitionem capere, et si ipsum inde culpabilem invenerit tunc liceat dictis servientibus seu ballivis suis dictum felonem super furcas dicti ducis de Halton suspendere, et bona et catalla dicti felonis infra feodum dominii sui predicti inventa habebit dictus dux sibi forisfacta ; et si dictus felo in nulla curiarum predictarum se ponere voluerit super inquisitionem ibidem, tunc mandetur ad castrum Cestrie et si ibidem dictus felo convictus fuerit, reducatur per servientes seu ballivos dicti ducis ad furcas ejusdem ducis de Halton, et ibidem suspendatur ; seu si finem inde fecerit domino comiti Cestrie tunc in utroque casu idem dux clamat omnia bona et catalla dicti felonis infra feodum dominii sui predicti inventa.

Item, clamat quod si vicecomes domini comitis Cestrie, vel aliquis serviens, in curia sua aliquem hominum dicti baronis inculpaverit, per thirtnyk se defendere poterit, nisi secta eum sequatur.[1]

Item, clamat habere quietanciam de garbis et oblationibus quas servientes et bedelli domini comitis Cestrie exigere solebant.

Ormerod, *Hist. of Cheshire*, ed. Helsby, i, 703–05, setting out the full plea, of which only extracts are given above.

[1] See footnote 1, p. 21, and No. 9 above.

No. 19

CHESHIRE.   The Serjeants of the Peace of the " Baron " of Dunham
           (see p. 21).

Hamo de Massie clamat . . . tanquam baro de Dunham . . .
habere vi servientes ibidem qui vocantur " serjiants of the peace "
qui servient curiae manerii predicti et facient attachiamenta et
executiones omnium placitorum et querelarum in dicta curia . . .
et de latronibus et de latroniis factis . . . ac habere ibidem puturam
servientium suorum predictorum de diversis tenentibus suis qui
tenent ibidem terram quam vocant terram puturæ.

Plea to *Quo Warranto, temp.* Edward III.   (Ormerod, i, 526 n.)

No. 20

CHESHIRE.   Order by Edward III to the justice of Chester as to
           the neglect of the Serjeants of the Peace in fee to
           perform their office.   1327 (see p. 23).

De servientibus pacis in comitatu Cestr'.   Rex dilecto & fideli
suo Ricardo Damory justiciario suo Cestr'.   Salutem.   Quia datum
est nobis intelligi quod servientes de feodo ad pacem nostram in
comitatu predicto conservendam constituti, ballivas suas aliis ad
terminum & alio modo dimiserint; quodque iidem servientes &
firmarii ea quæ ad conservacionem pacis nostræ pertinent minus
sufficienter excercent & diversa concelamenta de transgressionibus
illis contra pacem nostram factis faciunt; et quod vobis in conservacione pacis nostræ, prout decet, non intendunt, in nostri pre-
judicium & pacis nostræ læsionem manifestam; de quo admiramur
quamplurimum & movemur.   Nos, volentes pacem nostram illæsam
observari & perturbatores ejusdem puniri, prout decet, vobis
mandamus quod predictos servientes ex parte nostra premuniatis
quod ipsi vobis, in hiis quæ conservacionem pacis nostræ contingunt,
sint intendentes & quod pacem nostram in comitatu predicto,
prout ad officia sua pertinent, conservent; & si ipsos servientes,
post præmunicionem predictam, in premissis negligentes seu con-
trarios inveneritis, tunc ballivas illas in manum nostram capi &
eas salvo custodiri faciatis donec aliud inde a nobis habueritis in
mandatis.   T.R. apud Not' primo die Octobris.   Per ipsum Regem.

Close Roll 1 Edward III (1327); printed in Rymer, *Foedera*
(Rec. ed.), vol. ii, pt. ii, 717.

No. 21

CHESHIRE.   Commission to arrest malefactors.   19 Jan. 1391/2
           (see p. 26).

Commissio Radulfi de Vernon chivaler de malefactoribus arestandis.   Rex dilecto et fideli sui Radulfo de Vernon chivaler Salutem.
Quia ex gravi querela diversorum populi nostri comitatus Cestrie,
accepimus quod quamplures malefactores et pacis nostre perturbatores, tam de partibus externis quam intrincecis, vi et armis, videlicet
gladiis, peltis, baculis ferratis, arcubus et sagittis ac diversis aliis
armamentis, armati nocte dieque latitant et discurrunt in comitatu
nostro predicto in terrorem et affraiam populi nostri in eodem com-
morantis et pacis nostri perturbacionem manifestam ac in nostri

contemptu et contra proclamacionem nostram in hac parte factam. Assignavimus vos ad capiendum et arestandum omnes et singulos hujusmodi malefactores in terrorem seu affraiam populi nostri comitatus predicti vagantes, discurrentes, latitantes seu comitatum illum ingredientes, una cum armis suis quibuscunque, et ad illos ad castrum nostrum Cestrie ducendos et prisone nostre ibidem committendos et in eadem moraturos quousque de eorum deliberacione aliud duxerimus ordinandum. Damus autem universis et singulis maioribus, ballivis, ministris et aliis fidelibus et subditis nostris comitatus predicti tenore presencium firmiter in mandatis quod tociens quociens per vos ex parte nostra ad hoc faciendum debite fuerint premuniti, quod vobis ad officium vestrum juxta formam presentis mandati nostri faciendum intendentes sint obedientes et pro totis viribus suis auxiliantes. Proviso semper quod vos nobis de omnibus armis et armaturis virtute presentis mandati nostri per vos capiendis vel arestandis tamquam nobis forisfactis ad castrum nostrum predictum fideliter respondeatis. In cujus rei testimonium has litteras nostras fieri fecimus patentes quamdiu nobis placuerit duraturas. Datum apud Cestriam xix die Januarii anno regni regis quinto decimo. [19 Jan. 1391/2.] Consimilis commissio directa fuit Edwardo de Caryngton, Roberto de Mascy de Hale, Hamoni de Asshelegh et Hugoni de Mascy et unicuique eorum conjunctim et divisim sub dato tercio die Aprilis anno regni regis Ricardi secundi quintodecimo [3 April 1392].

Chester Recog. Roll, 2/64, m. 5 d (i).

No. 22

CHESHIRE. The first commission of *Conservatores pacis* in Cheshire, recited in letters of protection of 14 Aug. 1399 (see p. 27).

Henricus Percy, illustris domini Comitis Northumbr' primogenitus, Justiciarius Cestrie, omnibus infra hundredum de Edesbury residentibus et aliis quorum interest ad quos presentes littere pervenerint. Salutem. Cum metuendissimus dominus meus Henricus, Dux Lancastrie, Senescallus Anglie, communitatem Cestrie gratie sue benigne admiserit ac proinde volens pacem et tranquillitatem ubique infra eundem comitatum inviolabiliter custodiri, assignarit et constituerit dilectos sibi Ricardum de Wynynton chivaler et Ricardum de Manlegh, conservatores pacis in hundredo predicto, et ad publicam proclamacionem in locis in hundredo illo ubi melius expedire viderint nomine suo faciendam ne quis de aliis comitatibus eidem hundredo, vicinis et adjacentibus aut aliquis alius de partibus externis quicquam de bonis seu catallis quorumcumque hominum infra hundredum de Edesbury supradictum residencium contra voluntatem eorum capiat seu quovismodo capere presumat sub pena que incumbit, necnon ad omnes et singulos malefactores rebelles et pacis perturbatores infra hundredum illud inventos arestandos et capiendos et eos usque castrum Cestrie salvo duci faciendos, constabulario ejusdem castri ibidem liberandos et in eodem castro sub arta custodia moraturos quousque sufficientem securitatem de bono gestu suo in futuro invenerint, Suscepimus ipsos Ricardum et Ricardum, homines et servientes suos, terras, redditus, et omnes possessiones suas in proteccionem et defensionem nostras speciales. Et ideo vobis mandamus quod ipsos Ricardum et Ricardum manuteneatis, protegatis et defendatis, non inferentes eis vel inferri permittentes injuriam, molestiam, dampnum aut gravamen. Et si quid eis forisfactum fuit, id eis sine dilacione faciatis emendari. In cujus rei testimonium has litteras nostras fieri fecimus patentes quamdiu nobis placuerit duraturas; sigillo nostro proprio pro defectu sigilli officii nostri signatas. Datum apud Cestriam xiiii die Augusti anno regni regis Ricardi secundi vicesimo tercio. [14 Aug. 1399.] Per consilium. [Marginal heading.] Commissio custodum pacis in Hundredo de Edesbury.

Chester Recog. Roll, 2/94 (1 & 2 Henry IV), m. 3 (i).

No. 23

CHESHIRE. Commissions of *conservatores pacis* for all the Hundreds, 23 Jan. 1399/1400 (see p. 29).

Commissio custodum pacis. Henricus, filius illustris regis Anglie et Francie primogenitus, Princeps Wallie, Dux Aquitanie, Lancastrie et Cornubie, Comes Cestrie, dilectis et fidelibus suis Johanni de Pulle chivaler, Willelmo de Stanley, Hamoni de Masey, Johanni de Whitmore, Willelmo de Tranmoll, Jacobo de Pulle, Johanni Lytherlond, Johanni del Meoles, Thome de Bolde, Johanni de Teldesley, Viviano de Foxwyst et Gilberto Glegg et unicuique eorum conjunctim et divisim, Salutem. Quia diversi malefactores, pacis perturbatores et nobis rebelles, tam de civitate quam de comitatu nostris Cestrie, contra pacem nostram jam tarde vi armata apud Cestriam et alibi infra comitatum Cestrie insurrexerunt et se in routas, conventiculas et congregaciones illicitas et inhibitas aggregarunt, et diversas proclamaciones in diversis ecclesiis, villis, mercatoriis, foris mercatis et aliis locis infra comitatum predictum ex autoritate sua propria publice fecerunt quod omnes homines defensibiles ejusdem comitatus ad citius quo possent, omnibus aliis penitus relictis, sibi advenirent, sub pena vite, membrorum, tractus corporum, prostracionis domorum ac vasti et dilapidacionis bonorum suorum quorumcunque, ac plura que contra pacem nostram clare resonant, ut dicitur, facienda et sic coadunata sibi maxima fidelium nostrorum pre timore proclamacionum predictarum potestate, de locis in loca per comitatum predictum se diverterunt victualia, averia, bona, catalla et possessiones fidelium nostrorum communitatis populi comitatus predicti devastantes, destruentes et adnichilantes in nostri contemptum et communitatis populi nostri comitatus predicti dampnum non modicum gravamen et oppressionem et contra pacem nostram necnon communis insurrecionis tocius Anglie quod absit exemplum perniciosum, per quod tota communitas fidelium nostrorum comitatus predicti perturbata, inquietata et multipliciter fatigata fuit et commota. Nos pacem et tranquillitatem ubique in comitatu predicto confoveri et hujusmodi transgressores enormes rebelles et pacis perturbatores in eodem juxta eorum demerita puniri volentes, ut tenemur, constituimus vos et unumquemque vestrorum conservatores pacis nostre in hundredo de Wyrehale et ad ipsos omnes et singulos malefactores

qui primo sic contra pacem nostram hac vice vel antea insurrexerunt, necnon eorum fautores, receptores et mesprisionibus et
rebellioni eorundem consensientes ubicunque inventi fuerint in
hundredo aut comitatu predictis ubique arestandos, capiendos et
per corpora sua attachiandos et eos sic captos et arestatos de die
in diem usque castrum nostrum Cestrie salvo ducendos, constabulario nostro ibidem liberandos et sub arta custodia infra idem
castrum moraturos quousque de eorum deliberacione de assensu
consilii nostri duxerimus ordinandum. Et ideo vobis et unicuique
vestrorum mandamus firmiter injungentes quod circa premissa
omnia et singula de die in diem facienda et pro totis viribus vestris
ex parte nostra fideliter exequenda diligenter intendatis et ea
faciatis et exaquamini cum effectu. Et hoc sub fide et ligeancia
quibus dicto domino et patri nostri Regi supradicto et nobis tenemini,
ac sub pena omni quam penes nos forisfacere potetis nullatinus
omittatis . . .

Et qualiter presens mandatum nostrum fueritis executi scire
nobis faciatis et quilibet vestrorum scire faciat in scaccario nostro
Cestrie apud Cestriam in Octabis Purificacionis beate Marie jam
proximo futuris sub pena supradicta. In cujus rei testimonium has
litteras nostras fieri fecimus patentes quamdiu nobis placuerit
duraturas. Datum apud Cestriam xxiii die Januarii anno dicti
patris nostri Regis Henrici quarti post conquestum primo [23 Jan.
1399/1400]. Et talis commissio facta fuit cuilibet hundredo comitatus Cestrie diversis hominibus hundredorum illorum.

Chester Recog. Roll, 2/74, m. 3 d(i).

No. 24

CHESHIRE. Commission of a Bailiff Itinerant in the Counties of
Chester and Flint, 1362 (see p. 100).

Edwardus etc. Omnibus etc. Sciatis quod nos confidentes de
fidelitate et circumspeccione Hugonis de Pery constituimus eundem
Hugonem ballivum nostrum itinerantem in comitatibus nostris
Cestr' et Fflynt ad levandum omnes denarios nobis debitos in
eisdem comitatibus prout eidem Hugoni per camerarium nostrum
Cestr' et escaetorem nostrum Cestris' injungetur. Et ideo vobis
mandamus quod eidem Hugoni in premissis sitis intendentes et
respondentes. In cuius rei etc. Datum apud Cestriam die veneris
proximo ante festum Sancti Gregorii pape anno tricesimo sexto.
[1361–62.]

Chester Recog. Roll, 2/44, m. 3 (5).

No. 25

WALES. Charter of Henry III to the men of Englefield [Flints.]
granting various liberties, subject to an annual rent
and the finding of twenty-four serjeants of the peace.
5 May 1242 (see p. 33).

Grant to all the men of Englesfeld, dwelling without the King's
demesne lands of Englesfeld, that they and their heirs shall be
quit of the custom called " merchet " which they used to give
for marrying their daughters ; and of all food-rents (procurationibus)

and works of houses, which they used to render to Llewellyn, late prince of North Wales, and his men, and to David his son and his men ; and that they be subject to the King's court of Englesfeld according to the Welsh law and custom so that they shall not be drawn into plea of their lands and holdings without the King's land of Englesfeld, nor answer elsewhere than in the said court ; and their lands they shall hold of the King, rendering yearly by the hands of the bailiff of Englesfeld 50 *l.*, half at midsummer and half at the Exchequer of Michaelmas ; and finding twenty-four serjeants at their own cost to keep the peace in the land of Englesfeld ; saving to the King three mowings for three days in autumn from the men of Kayroys, Picton, Axton and the other towns of Englesfeld who are bound to do such mowings and did them in the time of Llewellyn and David.   Portsmouth, 5 May 1242.

Trans. in *Calendar Charter Rolls*, vol. i, 1226–57, pp. 274–75.

No. 26

WALES.   The collection, by the bedells of the commotes, etc., in Flintshire, of puture for serjeants, called *Porthiant cais.* 1301 (see p. 34).

De receptis Comitatus de Flynt.

De bedellis comoti de Coleshull pro putura servientium que vocatur Porthienkeys, solventibus per annum pro eadem ix *li.* xvij *s.* ij *d.* ad terminos Omnium Sanctorum et Invencionis Sancte Crucis, pro termino ultimo anni presentis xxix tantum quia [etc.] .   .   .   .   .   . iiii *li.* xviij *s.* vij *d.*

De bedellis comiti de Prestatton in Englefeld pro putura servientium [as above], solventibus per annum ix *li.* [as above].   .   .   .   . iiij *li.* x *s.*

De bedellis comoti de Rothelan pro putura servientium [as above], solventibus per annum vij *li.* xv *s.* [as above] lxxvii *s.* vj *d.*

De Blethino ap Ken', ballivo ville del Vaynol, pro porthienkeys quod est putura servientium, del Vaynol, de termino Assumptionis Beate Marie anno predicto pro toto anno   xxv *s.* vij *d.*

The first Chester Chamberlain's Account, 7 Feb. 1300/1–Mich. 1301.   (Wynnstay MS. 86, National Library of Wales.)   A similar but later account is in A. Jones, *Flint Ministers' Accounts.*

No. 27

NORTH WALES.   Extracts from the *Record of Caernarvon* relating to the Serjeants of the Peace (see p. 35).

In Recordis North Wallie continentur subscripta videlicet.

In primis per statutum de Rothelan Justiciarius North Wallie habet custodiam & gubernacionem pacis regie in North Wallia & terris Wallie adjacentibus ad justiciam quibuscunque exhibendam.

[1]   Item, inter ordinacionem pro pace in North Wallia de recordo reperitur quod ad instanciam & rogatum communitatis comitatus de Meryonnyth ordinatum & publice proclamatum fuit per Justiciarium quod conservatores pacis vocati keys

ammouerentur, et si aliqua felonia in eodem comitatu de die facta fuit et hutesium levatum et prosecutum, totus commotus in quo felonia sic facta fuit responderet de corporibus felonum vel de catallis depredatis et satisfaccione roborie, et hoc predicta communitas manucepit et similiter pacem domini servandam sub pena in recordis contenta. Et eodem modo in aliis comitatibus.

[2] Item, secundum antiquam legem Wallie in North Wallia conservatores pacis vocati keys fuerunt in omnibus comitatibus in North Wallia, quibusquidem keys tota patria per legem Wallie onerabatur invenire victum, pro quo ipsi keys custodirent patriam de malefactoribus et responderent de corporibus eorum et de eorum factis. Et quia tota patria senciebat se nimium gravatam de invencione poture et victus dictorum keys, ad peticionem communitatis tocius patrie keys ammoti fuerunt et pro ammocione tota patria manucepit pro pace ubique in North Wallia observanda et respondere de feloniis, depredacionibus et de corporibus malefactorum etc.

[3] Item, invenitur in diversis recordis quia diversa homicidia & roborie per malefactores & pacis perturbatores facta fuerunt in diversis locis infra comitatum Caernarvon, unde querimonia Justiciario cepius facta fuit per diversos patrie inde gravatos, Justiciarius pro pacis conservacione venire fecit coram eo omnes superiores & probiores Wallenses comitatus, plenam potestatem pro communitate tocius comitatus habentes, ad ordinandum & statuendum, una cum consilio dicti Justiciarii, super premissis remedium oportunum ; qui quidem probiores, per ordinacionem inter Justiciarium & ipsos factam, manuceperunt pro se et tota communitate comitatus pacem domini Regis in eodem comitatu conservare, et ordinaverunt custodes pacis in quolibet commoto, et pro eis manuceperunt quod nulli latrones, depredatores, homicide, malefactores aut pacis Regis perturbatores, indictati, utlagati aut notorii, intrinceci seu forinceci, receptabuntur cum ad eorum noticiam perveniunt, quin eos caperent seu de malefactis eorum responderent. Et postea predicta communitas, pro diversis murdris non presentatis & super communitatem adjudicatis & pro non conservacione pacis juxta ordinacionem antiquitus factam, & pro concelamento presentandi defaltas liberorum tenencium qui non veniunt coram Justiciario primo die itineris Justiciarii, amerciata fuit ad . . . CCCCV marcas, et sicut prius onerata fuit ad pacem conservandam juxta ordinacionem etc.

Communitas Wallensis comitatus de Meryonnyth pro eadem causa ad tantum amerciata fuit et onerata de conservacione pacis ut prius etc.

Communitas Wallensis comitatus Angles' eodem modo.

Record of Caernarvon, on ff. 131–32.

No. 28

WALES. Rents of the office of Serjeant of the Peace in the *Survey of Denbigh, 1334* (see p. 39).

Commote of Kaymergh [Cymeirch]. Officium seriantis pacis et satellitum valet per annum . . 32 *s.*
Commote of Rewaynok [Rhufoniog] Yssalet . 64 *s.*
  ,,   ,,   ,,   ,,   Yghalet . 40 *s.*
  ,,   ,, Roos Ysdulas . . . . . 60 *s.*
  ,,   ,,   ,, Ughdulas . . . . 106 *s.* 8 *d.*

Survey of Denbigh, 1334, ed. Vinogradoff & Morgan, 48, 152, 209, 270, 314.

No. 29

MONMOUTHSHIRE. Extract from charter of Walter de Lacy (d. 1241) to the Priory of Llanthony, giving acquittance from compulsory feeding of " keys " and other officers (see p. 44, n. 8).

Nolo etiam quod aliquis senescallus, constabularius, ballivus, keys, siue forestarius, serviens vel venator, vel aliquis ballivus alius per terram eorum venientes, ab ipsis nec ab hominibus suis pascantur nec aliquid cibi vel potus vel alterius rei ab eisdem canonicis vel hominibus suis accipiant nisi gratis dederint.

Dugdale, *Mon. Angl.* (1661 ed.) ii, 73 (wrongly numbered 71); (1830 ed.), vi, 138.

No. 30

LANCASHIRE. Charter of King John confirming previous grants of the hereditary master serjeanty of the hundred of West Derby, 1199 (see p. 50).

Confirmacio Henrici de Waleton honoris Lancastrie. Johannes Dei gratia Rex etc. Sciatis nos concessisse et hac carta nostra confirmasse Henrico filio Gilberti filii Walth' et heredibus suis sex bovatas terre in Waleton et iiii in Wauertre et iiii in Neusum et magistram sergentariam de wapentac', liberas et quietas per servicium sergentarie pro omni servicio et consuetudine in feudo et hereditate, tenandas de nobis et heredibus nostris libere [etc.] sicut Walthevus avus suus easdem terras et predictam sergentariam integre tenuit et habuit temporibus Willelmi comitis Bolonii Warrene et Moretonii et H. Regis patris nostri, et sicut easdem terras et eandem sergentariam Gilberto patri prefati Henrici concessimus et carta nostra confirmavimus dum comes Moretonii essemus. Teste [etc.] Datum [etc.] xxiii die Septembris anno regni nostri primo [1199].

Rot. Chart., 28.

No. 31

LANCASHIRE. The Serjeants of William de Ferrers, earl of Derby, 1251 etc. (see p. 51).

I.   Pro Comite de Ferariis. Rex concessit [*altered from* Mandatum est vicecomiti Lancastrie, quod permittat] Willelmo

de Ferrariis comiti Dereb' uni heredum Comitis Ranulfi quod
habeat servientes suos ad pacem conservandam inter Rybbel
& Meres' sicut predictus Radulfus quondam Comes Cestrie
tempore suo [*altered from* dum superstes fuit] illos habere
consuevit. Et mandatum est vicecomiti Lancastrie quod ipsi
eandem libertatem habere faciat, Et ipsum Comitem in eisdem
libertatibus et aliis quibus predictus Comes Randulfus tempore
suo usus est manuteneat & defendat. Teste Rege apud
Windles' xxix die Aprilis [1251] per ipsum regem. Postea
sic correctum fuit per Johannem de Lexinton'.
Close Roll, C. 54, 65 (35 Henry III), m. 14.

II. Pro Willelmo de Ferrariis Comite Dereb'. Vicecomiti Lancastrie Salutem. Quia concessimus per cartam nostram
dilecto & fideli nostro Willelmo de Ferrariis Comiti Dereb'
quod ipse & heredes sui habeant servientes suos ad pacem
nostram custodiendam inter Ribbel & Mers' sicut Ranulfus
quondam Comes Cestrie, cui predictam terram dedimus &
cujus unus heredum ipse est, eas habere consuevit, tibi precipimus quod predictum Comitem in libertate illa manutenens,
distringas homines illius patrie ad faciendum eisdem servientibus in victualibus & aliis ea que eis facere consueverunt tempore Comitis Cestrie predicti, ita in hiis exequendis te gerens
quod pro defectu tui ad nos inde querela non perveniat iterata.
Teste meipso ut supra [Teste Rege apud Clarendon ix die
Julii] [1252].
Close Roll, C. 54, 65 (36 Henry III), m. 10.

III. Lanc'. Willelmus de Ferrar' comes Dereb' attachietus fuit
ad respondendum Alano de Windhull & Thurstano de Holaunde
& aliis de placito quare vim facit predictis Alano & sociis suis
& illos distringit contra consuetudinem regni domini regis
ad recipiendum Grytsergeant in hundredo suo quem voluerit
illuc constituere, desicut nuper fuit convictum in curia domini
regis coram ipso domino rege per juratam de consensu partium
inter eos captam quod predictus Alanus & alii de hundredo
semper habuerunt talem libertatem quod ipsi consueverunt
& debuerunt, per consilium & consensum vicecomitis, eligere
Grytsergeanz & constituere, qui potuissent & debuissent
servare pacem domini regis & qui possent pro eis respondere
si pax domini regis non esset bene custodita, unde queruntur
quod dictus Willelmus Comes cepit & capi fecit averia ipsorum
Alani & aliorum circiter cc. & detinuit contra pacem etc.
unde dampnum etc. Et Willelmus per attornatum suum
venit & defendit vim etc. et quicquid etc. & dicit quod nec
cepit nec capi fecit averia predicta ea occasione & quod hoc
sit verum defendit contra ipsum Alanum & sectam suam.
Et quia sufficienter defendit consideratum est quod vadiat
legem etc. & veniat cum lege in crastino Ascencionis Domini
etc. Plegii de lege, Nicolaus Meurel & Petrus de Gatesden.
K.B. 26/152, m. 9, Hil. 38 Henry III (Jan.–Feb. 1253/4).

K

No. 32

LANCASHIRE.   The service of "witness" due from certain townships in the Wapentake of West Derby.   1346
(see p. 53).

Villata ibidem tenet de domino etc. in socagio ; debent etiam
sectam comitatus et wappentachie et poturam seruientium et ibunt
cum ballivis comitatus et wappentachie usque ad proximam villa-
tam ad testificandas districciones quociens et cum per cursum suum
acciderit cum aliis vicinis suis ; unde diversi tenentes tenent.

Extent of lands of earl of Lancaster 1346, in *Three Lancashire
Docts.*, Cheth. Soc., p. 30, and Farrer, *Lancs. Inquests, Extents*, &c.,
iii, 90, with very corrupt texts.

No. 33

LANCASHIRE.   Grant by King John of the hereditary Master Serjeanty of the Hundred of Salford.   1199 (see
p. 53).

Carta Elye filii Roberti honoris Lancastrie de sergentaria.

Johannes Dei gratia Rex etc.   Sciatis nos concessisse et presenti
carta nostra confirmasse Elye filio Roberti magistram sergentariam
de wapentach de Salford, habendam et tenendam de nobis et heredibus nostris sibi et heredibus suis, ita quod ipse Elyas et heredes
sui de omnibus exitibus de predicto wapentac' nobis et heredibus
nostris respondeant.   Quare volumus . . . quod idem Elyas et
heredes sui post ipsum habeant . . . predictam sergentariam per
predictum servicium sergentarie bene et in pace [etc.].

Teste [etc.].   Datum etc. x die Octobris [1199].

Rot. Chart., 27b.

No. 34

LANCASHIRE.   The Grith Serjeant of the "baron" of Manchester.
1322 (see p. 54).

The lord of Manchester has a liberty, namely infangenthefe,
utfangenthefe, tol and them, of the grant of the King . . . which
the lord of Mancestre and all his tenants are bound to hold ; where-
fore there is a certain bailiff, the lord's *serviens*, sworn to ride over
and watch over that lordship and to levy from the foreign tenants
the lord's rents and other things such as amercements and this
kind of thing if the lord's tenants have fallen into amercement,
and to summon or attach the transgressors against the said liberty
or otherwise, according to the manner of the offence ; who is called
gritheserjant which, being interpreted, is *custos pacis* ; and he
gives to the earl for his bailwick £10 one year with another, and
ought to be maintained with his groom and horses and four under-
bailiffs by the under-written tenants of the lord [*places named*] in
the lower bailiwick and upper bailiwick, who shall find for the said
master serjeant (*magistro servienti*) when he comes to them, bread,
ale and victuals and other necessaries according to season and for
his groom and four underbailiffs victuals according to those that
are provided in a household, and provender for his horse, upon

forewarning by any of them or by any messenger, of their coming.
And if distress or attachment should have to be made upon anyone in that lordship by any of the said bailiffs, each of those tenants,
if he be required for this, shall assist that serjeant to make the
said distress or attachment, and if a summons should have to be
made upon anyone, by anyone of them or distress should not be
permitted to him, each of those tenants who should have been
requisitioned for this shall furnish to the serjeant his testimony at
the court baron of Manchester; which custom is called "sarjantes
folde, bode and witnesse "; and if any tenant should make default
in any particular of the said custom, he ought to be impleaded by
the said serjeants in the said court and there make amends for the
offence.

Farrer, *Lancashire Inquests, etc.*, pt. ii, 66, being a translated
collation of various versions of an extent of the manor of Manchester 1322, the corrupt Latin texts of two versions of which are
printed in Harland, *Mamecestre*, 275 and 374.

No. 35

LANCASHIRE.   Charter of King John confirming his previous grant
of the hereditary master serjeanty of the Hundred
of Leyland.   1199 (see p. 54).

Confirmacio G. de Claitona de sergenteria.   Johannes Dei gratia
etc., Sciatis nos concessisse, dedisse et hac carta nostra confirmasse
Geroldo de Claitona pro homagio et servicio suo sergenteriam de
Leilondesir', habendam et tenendam ipsi Geroldo et heredibus suis
de nobis et heredibus nostris per servicium quod ad sergenteriam
illam pertinet nobis et heredibus nostris inde pro omni servicio
faciendum.   Quare volumus et firmiter precipimus quod idem G.
et heredes sui post ipsum habeant et teneant predictam sergenteriam
[etc.] sicut ei concessimus et rationabili carta nostra confirmavimus
dum comes Moretonii essemus.   Testibus [etc.].   Datum [etc.]
x die Octobris anno regni nostri primo [1199].

Rot. Chart., 27a.

No. 36

LANCASHIRE.   Charter of King John confirming his previous grant
of the hereditary master serjeanty of the Hundred
of Lonsdale.   1199 (see p. 55).

Johannes Dei gratia etc.   Salutem.   Sciatis nos concessisse et
hac carta nostra confirmasse Ade filio Ormi de Kellet serjantiam
de wapentac' de Lonesdal' cum tribus carrucatis terre in Kellet
pertinentibus ad serjantiam illam, tenendas de nobis et heredibus
nostris illi et heredibus suis.   Quare volumus et firmiter precipimus
quod idem Adam et heredes sui post ipsum habeant et teneant predictam terram cum omnibus pertinenciis suis per esse (ēe) serjantis
de eodem wapentac', libere et quiete [etc.] sicut ei concessimus et
carta nostra confirmavimus dum essemus comes Moretonii.   Teste
[etc.] Datum [etc.] xviii die Junii [1199].

Rot. Chart., xl.

No. 37

LANCASHIRE. The Grithserjeant of the Abbot of Furness, 1292
(see p. 56).

Assisa venit recognitura si Alexander de Kirkeby Irlyth, pater
Johannis de Kirkeby, . . . fuit seisitus . . . de manerio de Kirkeby
Irlith . . . quod abbas de Fournes tenet ; qui venit et dicit quod
ipse tenet duas partes prædicti manerii nomine custodie, ratione
minoris aetatis praedicti Johannis, quæ ad ipsum abbatem pertinent, eo quod predictus Alexander pater etc. tenuit prædictum
manerium de ipso abbate per homagium et fidelitatem et servitium
xxx solidorum per annum et faciendi arruras [et] syas et pascendi
grith servientem ipsius abbatis et faciendi sectam ad curiam
baroniæ suæ etc. [20 Edward I].

Furness Coucher Book, pt. ii (1887), 310. (The editor observed
that he had not in any other place met with the *grith* serjeant, or
with anything to throw light upon it.)

No. 38

WESTMORLAND. The powers of the Serjeant of the Peace over
the men of a " baron." 1278 (see p. 59).

Et quo ad hoc predicta communitas queritur quod ipse vicecomes
de feodo capere facit homines baronie predicte absque rationabili
causa et ipsos in prisona detinere quousque graves redemptiones
ab eis ceperit, dicit quod tempore Johannis regis avi domini regis
nunc quo tenuit comitatum istum in manu sua, usitatum fuit quod
si serviens juratus invenisset in baronia predicta aliquem hominem
suspectum de latrocinio seu de alio malefacto contra pacem, bene
liceret eidem servienti ipsum attachiare quod veniret ad proximum
comitatum postquam captus fuerat et ad tres comitatus post
captionem illam se essoniare et ad quartum apparere et tunc oportuit
ipsum ponere se in quatuor villas propinquiores loco ubi factum
quod ei inpositum fuerat fecisse debuisset et tunc oportuit ipsum
invenire plegios veniendi ad proximum comitatum auditurum
recognitionem villarum predictarum Et si aliquis sic captus per
suspicionem et veniendi ad comitatum plegios invenire non poterat,
tunc liceret servienti illi ipsum capere et ad prisonam ducere et
inprisonatum detinere usque ad deliberationem gayole . . .

Et Rogerus de Clyfford, vicecomes de feodo ratione Isabelle
uxoris sue aynecie, filie Roberti de Veteri Ponte quondam vicecomitis Westmerl' de feodo, venit et dicit quod ipse non clamat
nisi quatuor servientes, scilicet duos equites et duos pedites, in
baronia predicta ad facienda ea que ad dominum regem et vicecomitem pertinent et illi coram vicecomite in pleno comitatu sacra-
mentum prestarunt quod fideliter servient domino regi et populo
pertinenti baronie predicte. Et si plures sint servientes in baronia
predicta ipsos deadvocat.

From Assize Roll 982, m. 23 (7 Edward I), printed by Morris,
The Early English County Court, 158 and 172.

No. 39

WESTMORLAND.   Grant of lands by the " baron " of Kendal, free
from puture and " witnessman " for his land-
serjeants and foresters.   1220–46 (see p. 61).

Sciant etc. quod ego Willelmus de Lancastria dedi etc. Philippo
Coco meo . . . totam terram de Lintheued . . . et insuper Gres-
thwait etc.   Tenendam etc., in feodo etc., Ita videlicet quod idem
Philippus et hæredes sui quieti erunt de multura et de pannagio
et de pultura et withnesman landseriandorum et forestariorum
meorum et hæredum meorum inperpetuum.

Cockersand Chartulary, 1051.

No. 40

WESTMORLAND.   Charter of John de Vipont acquitting lords of
townships from maintenance of foresters etc.,
the lords to supply " witnessmen " for forest
offences on application (see p. 84).

Sciant presentes et futuri quod ego Johannes de Veteriponte
. . . concessi et quietum clamavi dominis de Sandford [and other
places] quietanciam de pultura forestariorum et de omnibus quæ
ego vel antecessores mei vel heredes vel forestarii mei aliquo tempore
occasione dictæ pulturæ capere vel exigere potuimus vel poterimus
testimonio veredariorum vel venatorum.   Ita tamen quod si forisfactum fuerit de foresta mea, vel de venatione vel de viridi vel de
forestar', inde venient ad supradictos dominos predictarum villarum
et petent ab eis *wytnesman,* et ipsi domini facient forestarios *wytnesman.*   Et omnes forestarii mei jurabunt invicem qui facti fuerint
forestarii quod nemini nocebunt occasione illius testimonii. [No
date given.]

Nicolson & Burn, *Hist. of Westmorland and Cumberland* (1777),
i, 23 n., from Machel MSS.   Cowell, *Interpreter* (1701), *s.v.* "witnesman," dates this charter 6 John and reads *facient forestarios
witnesman* which seems more likely than *facient forestariis wytnesman,* as in Nicolson and Burn.

No. 41

CUMBERLAND.   Acquittance by the lord of Millom to the abbey of
Furness, of puture for his sergeants and foresters
and of " bode " and " wynttenesman " from
land in Butterilket in Coupland.   1292 (see
p. 62).

Pateat universis . . . quod ego Johannes de Hodeleston concessi pro me et heredibus meis [etc.] in perpetuum quod abbas
Furnesiensis et ejusdem loci conventus [etc.] decetero sint quieti
de secta facienda ad curiam meam de Millum et etiam de pannagio
porcorum suorum et de putura forestariorum et servientium meorum
[etc.] et de bode et de wynttenesman inperpetuum, que servitia
quondam petii de predictis abbate et conventu pro terra sua de
Botherulkill in Coupland.

Furness Coucher Book, vol. ii, pt. 2, 539.

No. 42

NORTHUMBERLAND. The Chief Serjeant between Tyne and Coquet, 1259–60 (see p. 63).

Inquisicio facta de terris Nicholai de Bycre . . . anno regni regis xl quarto, coram Johanne de Kirkeby tunc excaetore domine regis in Norhambr' etc. . . . qui jurati dicunt quod dictus Nicholaus tenuit duas partes de Bycre etc. in capite de domino rege per seriantiam, ita quod capitalis serviens domini regis esse debet, ut predecessores sui fuerunt, ad instituendum et removendum omnes servientes inter Tinam et Koket. Sed hoc imbuit iniuste quidam vicecomes Philippus de Ulkotis et impedivit quod officium suum facere non potuit. Item dicunt quod idem Nicholaus custodire faciet averia capta pro debito domini regis in Norhambr' apud Bycre et, si averia sic capta moriantur, de coreis repondebit ad castellum domini regis in Norhumcastro et si vend' debeant pro dicto debito per visum ipsius vend' debent. Et idem Nicholaus deferre faciet brevia domini regis directa baronibus inter Tinam et Koket. Et quia predecessores sui feofaverunt quosdam de parte seriantie, videlicet de parvis messuagis, idem N. finem fecit cum domino rege pro xl solidis . . . Item jurati dicunt quod idem N. sepius faciebat officium coronarii inter Tinam et Koket cum coronarius interesse non potuit postea presentata re coronatoris, sed hoc imbuit Rogerus de Turkilby ad ultimum iter in Northumbr', quod ulterius non faceret [etc.].

Inquisitions post mortem, Henry III, No. 20, C. 132/23.

No. 43

SHROPSHIRE. Orders relating to the Serjeants of the Peace, 1220–24 (see p. 66).

(1) De servientibus Salop'. Rex abbati Salop' & Johanni Extraneo & omnibus de comitatu Salop' Salutem. Bene recolitis quod tempore domini J. Regis patris nostri constituti fuerunt servientes ad custodiendas partes Salopesbir'. Et quia postea partes ille gravate fuerunt ex multitudine illorum servientium, precepimus eos cum ultimo fuissemus Salop' amoveri usque ad numerum xii, gravaminibus vestris parcere volentes & expensis, sed nuper audivimus quod postea finem fecistis cum Henrico de Aldithel' per cc marcas ut penitus amoverentur servientes illi, unde vobis mandamus firmiter precipientes quatinus finem illum non observetis neque eidem Henrico reddatis sed sic ultimo constituimus permittatis servientes xii custodire partes vestras donec aliud inde providerimus & precepimus. Teste Rege etc. apud Ware primo die Julii [1220].
Patent Roll, 4 Henry III, C. 66/22, m. 4.

(2) De servientibus Salop'. Mandatum est Henrico de Aldithel' quod finem cc marcas, quem homines de comitatu Salop' cum eo fecerunt ut servientes constituti tempore J. Regis ad custodiendas partes Salop' penitus amoverentur, non observet nec recipiat, sed permittat xii servientes custodire partes illas

etc., sicut plenius continetur in rotulo Patencium. Teste H. etc.
apud War' j die Julie [4 Henry III, 1220].

Rot. Litt. Claus., i, 422a.

(3)   De servientibus Salop'. Rex Henrico de Aldithel' Salutem.
Mandamus vobis quod servientes, qui assignati fuerunt tempore
domini J. Regis patris nostri et postmodo in nostro tempore
usque ad festum Sancti Johannis Baptiste proximo preteritum
anno regni nostri quarto ad pacem conservandam in comitatu
Salop' pro malefactoribus parcium illarum, sine dilacione
penitus amoveatis, nec eos alicubi decetero admitti permittatis
ad sumptus alicujus in comitatu Salop' donec aliud inde precepimus. Teste H. etc. [apud Cantuar' ix die Julii] [4 Henry
III, 1220].

Rot. Litt. Claus., i, 423b.

(4)   De servientibus amovendis. Rex vicecomiti Salop' Salutem.
Precipimus tibi quod servientes qui assignati fuerunt tempore
domini J. Regis patris nostri et postmodum in tempore nostro
ad pacem custodiendam in comitatu Salop' pro malefactoribus
parcium illarum, decetero ibi esse non permittas, sed omnino
eos ammoveas donec aliud inde precepimus. Teste Rege [apud
Westmonasterium xxvi die Marcii anno regni nostri viii] [1224].

Rot. Litt. Claus., i, 589b.

No. 44

SHROPSHIRE. The imposition of Serjeants of the Peace in the
twelfth century (see p. 66).

Item, de consuetudinibus levatis, dicunt [juratores] quod Hugo
Puintulf posuit servientes ad voluntatem suam pro patria custodienda, et adhuc sunt in comitatu xij vel plus qui penitus vivunt de
hominibus patrie. Et milites de comitatu dicunt quod comitatus
emendaretur ad opus domini Regis si amoverentur. Et testatum
est quod Hugo primo apposuit eos pro terra sua custodienda
et postea attornavit ad comitatum custodiendum. [Margin]
Loquendum.

Placita apud Salopiam anno regni Regis Henrici sexto [1221–22],
printed in *Select Pleas of the Crown*, i, 110.

No. 45

SHROPSHIRE. Acquittance of the abbey of Shrewsbury from gifts
(*donerettum*) to future Grithserjeants. 20 June
1227 (see p. 67).

Rex etc. Salutem. Sciatis nos, intuitu Dei et pro salute anime
nostre et animarum antecessorum et heredum nostrorum, concessisse et presenti carta nostra confirmasse pro nobis et heredibus
nostris Deo et ecclesie beatorum apostolorum Petri et Pauli de
Salop' et abbati . . . et monachis ibidem Deo servientibus, quod
si aliquo tempore constituti fuerunt servientes in comitatu eodem
qui vocantur Grithserjanz donerant ad communem pacem conservandam, ipsi abbas et successores eius et . . . homines sui quieti
sint in perpetuum de doneretto predictorum servientium . . . ita
quod in terra predictorum abbatis et monachorum sive in terra

hominum suorum nullum decetero capient donerettum. [Grant also of a yearly fair.] Teste ut supra [apud Westmonasterium xx die Junii [1227]].

Charter Roll, 11 Henry III, pt. 1, C. 53/18, m. 1, no. 7.

No. 46

SHROPSHIRE. The ancient customary appointment and maintenance of Grithserjeants (see p. 67).

[p. 47.] Walterus de Bello Campo summonitus fuit ad respondendum Waltero de Hoptone de placito quare cepit averia ipsius Walteri de Hoptoni, etc. . . . apud Himestoke (etc.). . . .

[p. 49.] Et Walterus de Bello Campo venit et defendit vim etc. et dicit quod manerium de Wemme, cujus manerii Hymestoke est membrum, devenit in seisinam domini Regis post mortem cujusdam Gawyny le Botyler ratione minoris aetatis Willelmi fratris et heredis ejusdem Gawyny, cujus custodiam dominus Rex dedit Johanni de Britannia, et idem Johannes eandem custodiam dedit ipsi Waltero de Bello Campo, tenendam usque ad bonam aetatem predicti heredis. Et dicit quod antecessores ipsius heredis tali consuetudine usi sunt in eodem manerio quod licitum est ipsis ad conservationem pacis in partibus illis constituere servientes qui vocantur Grissergans [Grithserjauns *in Eyre Roll*] secumdum numerum majorem vel minorem prout ipsis antecessoribus melius esse videbatur; et quod predicti servientes debent sustentari per villanos manerii predicti et membrorum ejusdem manerii . . .

Et dicit quod villani de Hynestoke, quod est membrum de Wemme, contribuere solebant ad sustentationem praedictorum servientium . . .

[p. 53.] . . . paratus est verificare per quatuor etc. quorum primum est, scilicet, quod contributio integra ad sustentationem praedictorum servientium ad conservationem pacis domini Regis in partibus illis antiquitus concessa et ad communem utilitatem patriae ordinata est, quae dicitur servitium; et aliud est quod serjantia illa debeat reddi dominis de Wemme antecessoribus praedicti heredis apud Wemme quod est capitale messuagium baroniae prædictae [etc.].

Pleas in the Common Bench, 21 Edward I, 1293. *Year Book 21/22 Edward I* (Rolls Series), pp. 47, 49, 53.

No. 47

YORKSHIRE. Order exempting the men of the Knights Templars from the maintenance of the serjeants assigned to keep the peace. 1238 (see pp. 65, 71).

De hominibus Magistri Templi non distringendis. Mandatum est vicecomiti Eboraci quod non distringat homines Magistri Militie Templi in baillia sua ad dandum denarios in auxilium sustentationis servientum assignatorum ad conservationem pacis in partibus illis desicut homines sui parati sunt sicut et alii ad conservandum pacem regis quantum ad eos pertinet. T.R. apud Windles' xv die Julii [1238].

Close Roll, 1238.

No. 48

VARIOUS COUNTIES.   Order for the appointment of serjeants of the peace with pay from June to September 1241 (see p. 71).

Rex vicecomiti Ebor' salutem. Precipimus tibi quod, visis litteris istis, coram discretioribus et legalioribus militibus comitatus tui, de eorum consilio eligi facias viij servientes et eos retineatis ad equos et arma ad pacem nostram servandam, itineranda [sic] per diversas partes ejusdem comitatus secundum quod fuerit necesse, ita quod cum aliquid audierint vel sciverint de malefactoribus et perturbatoribus pacis nostre omnes villate vicine ad clamorem eorum super forisfacturam nostram veniant secundum quod singuli fuerint ad arma jurati, et una cum predictis servientibus ipsos malefactores et perturbatores insequantur quousque capiantur. Et cum tales capti fuerint vel alii de quibus habita sit mala suspicio, tu eos sine omni occasione et difficultate recipias et salvo custodias in prisona nostra donec a nobis aliud habueris mandatum. Et ne probi homines nostri de comitatu tuo per predictos servientes et homines eorum aliquo modo graventur, singulis eorum habere facias in die de bursa nostra vj denarios ad sustentationem suam, equi, et hominis sui a die qua hec provisio facta fuerit, que fiat citra Dominicam proximam ante festum Sancti Barnabe Apostoli, usque ad Exaltationem Sancte Crucis, quod quidem tibi faciemus allocari. Fieri etiam facias vigilias in singulis villis comitatus tui usque ad festum Sancti Petri ad Vincula secundum quod alias fieri preceperimus. Et vigiles ita sint diligentes in arestandis malefactoribus quod nullus extraneus vel alius de quo mala suspicio habeatur transire possint [sic] quin arestetur usque ad diem. Et tu de premissis ita diligenter te intromittas ne ad te pro defectu tui vel ad predictos servientes, quorum nomina nobis scire facias, nos graviter capere debeamus. T.R. xxviij die Maii [1241].

Sussex' Kancia	} Willelmus de Casingham cum vj. servientibus.
Essex'	cum iiij servientibus.
Hertford' Norf' Suff'	} cum iiij ,,
Norht' Buk' Bedeford' Glouc' Linc'.	} cum vj.
Oxon' Berk' Warewik Leyc' Wigorn' Hereford' Notingham Dereby	} cum iiij.

Close Roll, 1241.

No. 49

STAFFORDSHIRE. Order for the maintenance of six Serjeants of
the Peace with pay from April to August 1242
(see p. 71).

De servientibus ad pacem regis custodiendam. Mandatum est
custodi episcopatus Cestrensis quod provideat de sex servientibus
qui melius possint et velint custodire pacem regis in comitatu
Stafford' et singulis eorum faciat habere unum denarium in die a
Pascha anno, etc. xxvj [1242] usque ad festum Sancti Petri ad
Vincula [1 Aug.] anno eodem, et rex denarios ipsos ei faciet allocari.
T.R. xiiij die Aprilis [1242].

Close Roll, 1242.

PRINCIPAL PRINTED SOURCES AND AUTHORITIES CITED

Ancestor, The, vol. i, 1902.

Anderton, " A Blackburnshire Puture Roll " (*Trans. Hist. Soc. Lancs. & Chesh.*, 64, 273).

Archæologia Cambrensis, various vols.

Attenborough, *Laws of the Earliest English Kings*, 1922.

Ault, *Private Jurisdiction in England* (Yale Hist. Publn., 1913).

Baines, *History of Lancashire* (several editions).

Bateson, *Borough Customs* (Selden Soc., 2 vols., 1904–06).

Beard, *Office of Justice of the Peace in England* (Columbia Univ. Studies in Hist., xx, 1904).

Black Prince's Register (P.R.O.), 4 vols., 1930, etc.

Bolland, *The Eyre of Kent 1313–14* (Selden Soc., 1910–13).

Book of Fees (Testa de Nevill) (P.R.O.).

Bromfield and Yale, Extent 1315, ed. Ellis (Soc. of Cymmrodorion, Rec. Ser. xi).

Caernarvon, Sheriff's Account, 1303–04 (Bulletin Board of Celtic Studies, vii, 143).

Calendars, P.R.O. :
  Charter Rolls.
  Close Rolls.
  Inquisitions.
  Patent Rolls.
  Cheshire Pleas Rolls (26–30 Reps. D.K.).
  Cheshire Recognisance Rolls (36, 37, 39 Reps. D.K.).

Calendar Chester County Court Rolls, 1259–97, ed. R. Stewart-Brown, 1925 (Cheth. Soc., N.S., 84).

Cam, *Studies in the Hundred Rolls* (Oxford Studies in Social and Legal History, vol. vi).

Chamberlain's Account for North Wales, 1304, trans. by E. A. Lewis (Bulletin Board of Celtic Studies, i, 256).

Cheshire Chamberlains' Accounts, 1301–60, ed. R. Stewart-Brown, 1910 (Rec. Soc. L. & C., 59).

Cheshire Inquisitions post mortem, ed. R. Stewart-Brown, 1934 (Rec. Soc. L. & C., 84).

Cheshire Sheaf, various volumes.

Chester Abbey, Chartulary of, ed. Tait (Cheth. Soc., N.S., 79, 82).

Chester Archæological Soc., *Journals*.

Chirk Castle and Chirkland, Mahler, 1912.

Chirkland, Extent, 1391–3, ed. Jones, 1933.

Chronicon Adæ de Usk, 2nd ed., 1904.

Cockersand Abbey, Chartulary of, ed. Farrer (Cheth. Soc., N.S., 7 vols., 1898–1909).
Coke, *Institutes.*
Cowell, *Interpreter,* 1701.
Cox, *Royal Forests of England,* 1905.

Domesday Survey of Cheshire, ed. Tait (Cheth. Soc., N.S., 75).
Dowdell, *A Hundred Years of Quarter Sessions,* 1932 (Cambridge Studies in Eng. Legal Hist.).
Du Cange, *Glossarium.*
Du Moulin, *Coustumes Generales . . . de France,* 1664.
Dugdale, *Baronage,* 1675.
—— *Mon. Anglicanum,* 1661 and 1817–30.

Early Eng. Text Soc., " The Lay of Havelock the Dane," 1868.
Earwaker, *East Cheshire* (The Hundred of Macclesfield), 1878.
English Historical Review, various articles.

Farrer, *Records of Kendale.*
——, " Notes on Domesday Survey " (*Lancs. and Chesh. Antiq. Soc., xvi*).
Flint Ministers' Accounts, ed. Jones (Flint Hist. Soc., 1913).
Flint Pleas, 1283–5, ed. Edwards (Flint Hist. Soc., 1922).
Furness Coucher Book (Cheth. Soc., N.S., 9, 11, 14, 74, 76, 78).

Hale, *Pleas of the Crown.*
Harland, *Three Lancashire Documents* (*Survey of 1320–46*) (Cheth. Soc., O.S., 74).
——, *Mamecestre* (Cheth. Soc., O.S., 53, 56, 58).
Haskins, *Norman Institutions,* 1918.
Hazeltine (H. D.), Gen. Preface on the historical development of the Justice of the Peace, in Dowdell, *A Hundred Years of Quarter Sessions,* 1932.
Hearnshaw, *Leet Jurisdiction in England,* 1908.
Heginbotham, *Stockport,* 1882.
Historic Society of Lancs. and Chesh., *Transactions.*
Holdsworth, *A History of English Law,* 5th ed. (9 vols.), 1931, etc.
Hulton, *Priory of Penwortham* (Cheth. Soc., O.S., 30).

Jolliffe, " Era of the Folk in English History " (*Oxford Essays presented to H. E. Salter,* 1934).
——, " Northumbrian Institutions " (*Eng. Hist. Review,* 41, 1926).

Lancashire Assize Rolls, ed. Parker (Rec. Soc. L. & C., 47, 49).
Lancashire Court Rolls, ed. Farrer (Rec. Soc. L. & C., 41).
Lancashire Fines, ed. Farrer (Rec. Soc. L. & C., 39, 46, 50).
Lancashire Inquests and Extents, ed. Farrer (Rec. Soc. L. & C., 48, 54, 70).
Lancashire and Cheshire Star Chamber Cases, ed. R. Stewart-Brown (Rec. Soc. L. & C., 71).
Lapsley, " Buzones " (*Eng. Hist. Review,* 47, 1932, p. 556).
——, *County Palatine of Durham,* 1900.

Lapsley, " Parliamentary Title of Hen. IV " (*Eng. Hist. Review*, 50, 1935).
Letters and Papers, Foreign and Domestic, Henry VIII.
Liebermann, *Constitutiones de Foresta*, 1894.
——, *Die Gesetze der Angelsachsen*, 1898, etc.
Lloyd, *History of Powys Fadog*, 1881.
Lysons, *Cheshire*, 1810.

McKechnie, *Magna Carta*, 2nd ed., 1914.
Maitland, " Criminal Liability of the Hundred " (*Collected Papers*, vol. i).
——, *Domesday Book and Beyond*, 1897.
——, *Justice and Police*, 1885.
——, " Outlines of English History " (*Collected Papers*, vol. ii).
Medieval Latin Word-List, 1934.
Merioneth, Survey of (Arch. Cambr., iii, vol. 12).
Morris (R. H.), *Chester in Plantagenet and Tudor Reigns* [1895].
Morris (W. A.), *Early English County Court*, 1926 (California Univ. Publs. in Hist.).
——, *Frankpledge System*, 1910 (Harvard Univ. Hist. Study xiv).
——, *Mediaeval English Sheriff*, 1927.

Nicolson and Burn, *Westmorland and Cumberland*, 1777.
Northumberland, A History of, 1893, etc.
Northumberland, Three Assize Rolls (Surtees Soc., 88).

Ormerod, *History of Cheshire*, 1817 ; ed. Helsby, 1882.

Palgrave, *English Commonwealth*, 1832.
Palmer (A. N.), *Ancient Tenures in North Wales*, 1885.
——, " Town of Holt " (*Arch. Cambr.*, 1906–10).
——, " Two Charters of Henry VII " (*Y Cymmrodor*, xix).
Palmer and Owen, *Ancient Tenures in North Wales*, 2nd ed., 1910.
Petit-Dutaillis, *Studies Supplementary to Stubbs' Constitutional History*, ed. Tait, 1908–14 (1915).
Pipe Rolls, Henry I, Henry II, Richard I, John, pr. 1833–44.
Pipe Roll Society, Publications (various).
Pipe Roll 26 Henry III, ed. Cannon.
Placita de Quo Warranto, 1818.
Placitorum . . . Abbreviatio, 1811.
Pollock and Maitland, *History of English Law, etc.*, 2nd ed., 1911.
Porteus, *The Hundred of Leyland* (Cheth. Soc., N.S., 90).
Putnam, *Early Treatises on the Justices of the Peace*, 1924 (Oxford Studies in Social and Legal Hist., vol. 7).
——, " Enforcement of the Statutes of Labourers " (*Columbia Univ. Study in Hist.*, 32, 1908).
——, " Records of the Keepers of the Peace, 1307–27 " (*Eng. Hist. Review*, 45, 1930).
——, " Transformation of Keepers of the Peace into the Justices of the Peace " (*Trans. Royal Hist. Soc.*, 1929).
——, " Kent Keepers of the Peace, 1316–17 " (*Kent Arch. Soc.*, 1933).

Record of Caernarvon (Rec. Comm.), 1838.
Rees, *South Wales and the March, 1284–1415,* 1914.
Reid, " Barony and Thanage " (*Eng. Hist. Review,* 35, 1920).
Robertson, *Laws of Kings of England from Edmund to Henry I,* 1925.
Rotuli Chartarum, 1837 (Rec. Comm.).
Rotuli Hundredorum, 1812–18 (Rec. Comm.).
Rotuli Literarum Clausarum, 1204–27 (Rec. Comm.), 1833–44.
Rotuli Parliamentorum.
Round, " Burton Abbey Surveys " (*Eng. Hist. Review,* 20, 1905).
——, *The King's Serjeants,* 1911.
Rymer, *Fœdera* (Rec. ed.).

St. Bees, Register of Priory of (Surtees Soc. 126).
Select Pleas of the Crown, 1220–25, ed. Maitland (Selden Soc., 1888).
Skeel, *The Council in the Marches of Wales,* 1904.
Statutes of the Realm (Rec. Comm.), 1810–28.
Stewart-Brown (R.), " Avowries of Cheshire " (*Eng. Hist. Review,*
    29, 1914).
——, " Cheshire Pleas of *Quo Warranto,* 1499 " (*Eng. Hist. Review,*
    1934, and *Cheshire Sheaf,* 1935).
——, " End of the Norman Earldom of Cheshire " (*Eng. Hist.
    Review,* 35, 1920).
——, " Suete de Prisone " (*Eng. Hist. Review,* 24, 1909).
——, " Thwert-ut-nay and the Custom of Thwertnic in Cheshire "
    (*Eng. Hist. Review,* 40, 1925).
——, *The Wapentake of Wirral, A History of the Hundred Court,* 1897.
Stubbs, *Constitutional History of England,* library ed., 3 vols., 1880.
——, *Select Charters,* 9th ed.

Tait, *Mediæval Manchester and the Beginnings of Lancashire,* 1904.
Tout, " Flintshire " (*Jour. Flint. Hist. Soc.,* 1911).
Tupling, *Economic History of Rossendale* (Cheth. Soc., N.S., 86).
Turner, " Bookland and Folkland " (*Historical Essays in Honour of
    James Tait,* 1933).
——, *Select Pleas of the Forest* (Selden Soc., 1901).

Vale Royal Abbey, Ledger Book of, ed. Brownbill (Rec. Soc. L. & C.,
    68).
Victoria County Histories, especially Lancashire, Cumberland and
    Westmorland.
Vinogradoff, *English Society in the Eleventh Century,* 1908.
——, *Growth of the Manor,* 2nd ed., 1911.
——, *Villainage in England,* 1892.
—— and Morgan, *Survey of the Honour of Denbigh, 1334,* 1914.

Waters, *The Edwardian Settlement of North Wales, 1284–1343,* 1935.
Wetheral Priory Register, ed. Prescot, 1897.
Whalley Abbey Coucher Book, ed. Hulton (Cheth. Soc., O.S., 10, 11,
    16, 20).

Y Cymmrodor.
Year Book 21–22 Edward I (Rolls Series).
Yorkshire, Early Charters, II, ed. Clay (Yorks. Arch. Soc., Rec. Series).

INDEX OF PERSONS AND PLACES

L

SUBJECT INDEX

Printed in Great Britain by Butler & Tanner Ltd., Frome and London